WHY SEND YOUR CHILD TO A CATHOLIC SCHOOL?
EDITED BY MAURA HYLAND

WHY SEND YOUR CHILD TO A CATHOLIC SCHOOL?

Edited by
Maura
Hyland

VERITAS

Published 2013 by
Veritas Publications
7–8 Lower Abbey Street
Dublin 1, Ireland
publications@veritas.ie
www.veritas.ie

ISBN 978 1 84730 520 6

A catalogue record for this book is available from the British Library.

Designed by Heather Costello, Veritas Publications
Printed by Gemini International, Dublin

Veritas books are printed on paper made from the wood pulp of managed forests.
For every tree felled, at least one tree is planted, thereby renewing natural resources.

Contents

Preface

Maura Hyland

The debate about denominational education and its future in Ireland is high on both the political and religious agendas right now. Decisions are being made that will have a lasting effect on the choices that will be available for parents when deciding where to send their children to school. Parents are the first and most important educators. When the time comes to choose a school, parents' wish is that all they are already passing on to their children in the home will be affirmed and continued in the school they choose.

There are many things that set each school apart – among them, the quality of the education it delivers and the sort of place it is for children to inhabit. Schools name the second of these as their 'characteristic spirit'. Every school's characteristic spirit is different, depending on the tradition in which the school was established, where the school is situated, and who its students and teachers are. For Catholic schools, however, characteristic spirit is always influenced by the teaching of Jesus. Catholic schools strive to be places where children learn how to live with others in a way that is shaped by how Jesus lived with and treated others.

This book is addressed to parents who are wondering what difference sending their children to a Catholic school might make. Ultimately, every parent has to decide which school to choose for their children – this book provides a variety of insights into why a Catholic school could be a good choice.

Introduction

Michael Drumm

Schools are important places. We spend a lot of time in them. This includes a significant proportion of that most formative period in life between four and eighteen years of age. The informal education received at home and in the community is of crucial significance. The formal education of children in schools has its own integrity related to the stage of development of the pupils. When schools are working at or near their best they are truly a remarkable human achievement. Young children have a safe place to learn and play and pray; adolescents grow into a deeper intellectual, emotional and moral world; teachers use their personal and professional abilities to nurture and challenge new generations; parents, members of boards of management and other adults give of their time and money to support the educational enterprise. The hope is that by eighteen a young adult who is free, rational and capable of mature relationships will be able to cross the threshold into higher education or the world of work. So, why choose a Catholic school?

Well, first it must be acknowledged that all schools hold much in common in terms of structures, curriculum, inspection and assessment. Every school attempts to serve society in a meaningful way. While a large percentage of schools are under the patronage of the Catholic Church, these schools, like all schools in the Republic of Ireland, are effectively governed by the State through the Department of Education and Skills (DES). The DES strictly regulates the curriculum of schools through the National Council for Curriculum and

Assessment and the inspectorate's Whole School Evaluation processes. Section 30 of the Education Act (1998) states that the Minister determines:

a. the subjects to be offered in recognised schools;
b. the syllabus of each subject;
c. the amount of instruction time to be allotted to each subject;
d. the guidance and counselling provision to be offered in schools.

Schools must comply not only with extensive legislation but also with the multitude of circulars and guidelines, which issue from the Department of Education and Skills. Given that so much of what is done in school is determined by the State, what difference does it make which school a child attends?

The answer is found in the ethos or characteristic spirit of the school, and every school has its own. In the Education Act 15 (2) (b) the characteristic spirit of the school is understood as being 'determined by the cultural, educational, moral, religious, social, linguistic and spiritual values and traditions which inform and are characteristic of the objectives and conduct of the school'. It is clear from this that Catholic schools will vary depending on their history and the sociodemographic realities of the communities they serve. Yet, from the small rural school serving a whole community to the large urban school serving a very diverse population, all such schools are challenged to give expression to their characteristic spirit through the lens of Catholic faith. This should not be understood as something static or oppressive; rather it is best understood as an invitation to allow Catholic faith to inform the values and traditions that are lived out on a daily basis in the school.

Schools today find themselves in challenging circumstances due to enormous social, cultural and economic changes. In an age dominated by media and information technology and during a serious economic recession, significant new pressures are brought to bear on children and adolescents, on family structures, on religious practice, on community life and, not least, on behaviour in the school classroom. In this new cultural context every school needs to redefine its identity, so that it is not just reacting to the latest trend or fashion but that it can truly articulate its self-understanding. This is a challenge that Catholic schools take seriously.

In giving expression to their ethos Catholic schools attempt to live out the following principles:

» Catholic schools continue the work of Jesus the teacher;
» Catholic schools are part of a living tradition;
» Catholic schools respect both faith and reason;
» Catholic schools incarnate the spirit of the Second Vatican Council.

Schools guided by these principles provide an intellectually stimulating and spiritually nurturing environment for all children who attend them.

Catholic Schools Continue the Work of Jesus the Teacher

Jesus is called 'teacher' on forty-six occasions in the gospels. It is the title most commonly associated with him by his first disciples. So what did Jesus teach? In the villages, hills and valleys of Galilee he taught the people that the reign of God was dawning in their midst. He spoke of the reign of God as healing for the sick, hearing for the deaf, new sight for the blind, freedom for prisoners, good news for the poor. He revealed a deeper communion with God through ordinary human realities. In Matthew's gospel alone he speaks of mothers, fathers, husbands, wives, widows, sons, daughters and children; alms, bankers, burglars, coppers, debts, deposits, employment, merchants, money, gold, silver, purses, taxes, tenants, thieves and wages; birds, cattle, chickens, donkeys, fish, foxes, goats, hens, moths, oxen, pigs, sheep and snakes; corn, figs, fields, flowers, grapes, flour, loaves, logs, plants, roots, reeds, salt, seed, thistles, thorns, trees, weeds, vineyards, wheat and harvest; banquets, weddings, brides, bridegrooms, dancing, pipes, dinners and feasts; and that still leaves clothes, boats, fires, floods, footwear, gales, lamps, haversacks, nests, nets, oil, rain, shepherds, reapers, splinters, sunset, tunics, woodworm and yeast. And, yes, he did speak about the weather!

A key element of the Christian message is that life is not the way it was intended to be. It is broken in all sorts of ways. Your life and mine, our families, and, yes, our schools and all our relationships are fraught with human limitations. Christian discipleship is characterised by healing, hearing, new sight, freedom and good news. But to grasp in a deeper way what these liberating possibilities mean we need to become aware of the realities of sickness, deafness, blindness, captivity and poverty. When we look honestly at ourselves and those around us we discover that we are the sick, the deaf, the blind, the captive, the poor – and not just in a metaphorical sense but in the physical, psychological and spiritual realities of our lives. Only when we immerse ourselves in these human experiences can we discover who Jesus really was, for his ministry was all about lifting burdens. Whether the burdens were created by selfishness or laziness or a scrupulously strict religious sensibility or blind obedience or political corruption or grinding poverty or sickness or lack of self-esteem or pride or prejudice, the result was the same: people were in need of healing.

The call of Christian discipleship demands that we always seek to lift the burden. Whether this means helping people to stand up and walk on their own, exorcising their fear of the unknown, expanding their minds through education, feeding them when they are too weak to feed themselves, opening their eyes to the reality of life, challenging them to let go of hurts and prejudice, liberating those who are unjustly oppressed, introducing them to ever greater horizons of transcendence and beauty, unsealing their ears to hear the divine echo in their hearts, unleashing their hope for the future, or sowing the seeds of eternal life, the healing ministry of Jesus is continued as 'the blind see again, the lame walk, lepers are cleansed and the deaf hear, the dead are raised to life, the good news is proclaimed to the poor' (Lk 7:22). To teach as Jesus taught means inviting people to live without crutch or grudge or closed mind. Christian education invites people to become Christlike in their lives so that the reign of God might continue to dawn in our world.

Notice that all of Jesus' teaching takes place through the words that he speaks and the encounters that are at the centre of his ministry. To teach as Jesus taught is surely to speak words of honesty, words of forgiveness, words of compassion; and it is to encounter people wherever they are and invite, cajole and liberate them to move on. Think of the Samaritan woman at the well, little Zacchaeus in Jericho, Matthew the tax collector in Capernaum, the two disciples on the road to Emmaus, Mary from the town of Magdala at the tomb on Easter Sunday morning – all people totally preoccupied with their own worries and concerns but who are challenged to move on through their encounter with Jesus. This teaching is truly education – to lead people out of ignorance, out of hostility, out of self-centredness, out of fear, into somewhere new. Such education is an endless task in all of our lives. Catholic schools are committed to continuing this ministry of Jesus.

Catholic Schools are Part of a Living Tradition

Schools with a religious ethos exist in almost all countries except those where they are outlawed by non-democratic regimes. In many nations, as in Ireland, they form a central part of the education system; while in almost all democratic societies they are funded by the State. Such schools provide a real public service and they are a notable expression of the contribution of the voluntary sector to the development of a vibrant civil society. The interaction between religious belief and education is as old as schooling itself. From the schools and universities of medieval Europe, through the growing rates of literacy promoted by the Reformation and Counter-Reformation in the sixteenth and seventeenth centuries, and on to the large number of Catholic schools throughout the world in the twenty-first century, Catholic tradition is inseparable from education.

So why has the Catholic Church been so involved in schools, colleges and universities? Because Christians, from the beginning, wanted to hand on their treasured tradition. Jesus proclaimed the reign of God. The early Christians believed that the decisive breakthrough of God's reign in history occurred in the death and resurrection of Jesus Christ. Thus the messenger became the message, the preacher became the preached, the proclaimer became the proclaimed. From the beginning, Christians gathered to celebrate this mystery of Christ. They listened to God's word as it was proclaimed to them from the scriptures and they shared in the breaking of the bread. In doing these actions they believed the Lord to be especially present in their midst. This tradition has been handed down from generation to generation of Christians, from parents to children to children's children, right down to us today. And we will hand it on to the generations coming after us. This is what it means to be part of tradition: we receive it rather than create it; we cherish it and we hand it on in trust to those who will follow us. It forms us more than we form it. It gives our lives a story, a texture, a value which is more than the story of our own families, more than the texture of our own experience, more than the values that we could work out for ourselves. Thus the reality of tradition became central to Christian identity and it is the bedrock for Catholic schools. It is like the sensible person who builds the house on rock. The rain, floods and gales that inevitably come will not prevail. Schools that are embedded in Catholic tradition and seek to live it for our times are a key part of the life of the Church.

Catholic Schools Respect Both Faith and Reason

There is a temptation in contemporary Irish discourse to dismiss religious belief as inherently irrational, divisive and anti-intellectual. Some go so far as to say that schools with a Catholic ethos cannot create a sense of civic virtue. This runs completely contrary to the Catholic education tradition, which is built on a respect for faith and reason. Those who dismiss schools with a religious ethos as little more than proselytising and indoctrinating tools of religious authorities show little sense of the long evolution of Catholic schools over many centuries, the rich diversity within the Catholic sector and the principles which underpin such education today. The most important principle of all is the value placed on both faith and reason. It is this principle which helps to explain why Catholic schools are so popular and respected throughout the world.

In an era often dominated by religious fundamentalism on the one hand and atheistic science on the other, this commitment to a dialogue between faith and reason was rarely more relevant. We live in an era when science and religion might completely diverge from each other, as if it was impossible for the same person to be a rigorous scientist and a sincere religious believer. Faith and reason can live and thrive in the same person: while one cannot be reduced to the other, they both play a dynamic role in forming and educating a mature person. There is no contradiction between being a fully educated person and a committed Christian. There are few more important tasks for Christian educators than to revisit and reimagine the relationship between faith and reason.

Pope Benedict XVI has consistently drawn attention to this fundamental issue. At his meeting with representatives of British society in Westminster Hall he said:

I would suggest that the world of reason and the world of faith – the world of secular rationality and the world of religious belief – need one another and should not be afraid to enter into a profound and ongoing dialogue, for the good of our civilization.[1]

Catholic schools and colleges are called to live out this dialogue every day.

Catholic Schools Incarnate the Spirit of the Second Vatican Council

Though it took place some fifty years ago, the teaching and pastoral insights of the Second Vatican Council are still being received and interpreted in the broader Catholic community. The Council heralded a new openness to the modern world which has been expressed most forcibly through various dialogues: with other Christians, with people of other faiths and with non-believers. The most powerful symbolic expression of these dialogues has been in Assisi, where Pope John Paul II and Pope Benedict XVI gathered with leaders of Christian Churches and of other faiths. These dialogues take place at various levels, from international gatherings to local communities, from universities to schools and colleges. The most important dialogue is that between faith and reason.

Pope Benedict XVI described the Second Vatican Council as dedicated to finding a new definition of the relationships between the Church and the modern age, between the Church and the modern state and between Christian faith and other religions.[2] Catholic schools and colleges are continually reinterpreting these various

---

1   Pope Benedict XVI, Meeting with the Representatives of British Society, Including the Diplomatic Corps, Politicians, Academics and Business Leaders, Westminster Hall (17 September 2010).

2   Address of His Holiness Benedict XVI to the Roman Curia (22 December 2005).

relationships as they live out the interface between Catholic faith and modern science. They are a living expression of the interaction between Catholic institutions and democratic governments, and they are a context for the daily encounter with those of other faiths and none.

The ongoing reception and interpretation of Vatican II now takes place in the context of the ministry of Pope Francis. He has challenged all members of the Church to reach out again to the world, not least to those who are on the margins of society. He speaks of two temptations: that of seeking to return to a past which no longer exists and that of embracing every secular trend. In contrast, he calls Christians to live out their faith in the world in which they find themselves. Hopefully, the ministry of Pope Francis will give renewed energy to Catholic schools as they incarnate the spirit of Vatican II, in creating a mature relationship with modernity, in seeking to be active participants in democratic societies and in fostering dialogue between all people of goodwill.

Different Perspectives

In this book there are six different perspectives given on the benefits and features of a Catholic education. Bishop Donal McKeown challenges all involved in Catholic schools to imagine a new future. He wants Catholic schools to be much more than just very good at secular education. This 'more' must be imagined and lived in new ways and he provides many helpful suggestions about how this might be done.

Baroness Nuala O'Loan speaks of the influence of her Catholic schooling on her own life. She emphasises the formative power of the people she met that bore witness to their own faith:

It was not just their kindness, their humanity, their goodness; it was their faith – so much more profound than goodness –

which helped me to comprehend the presence of God in my life and helped me in the journey to know, love and serve [God] in all that I do and with all whom I meet. This is the essence of my existence.

Amalee Meehan reflects on the Catholic school's characteristic spirit, God as Mystery, God as Love, Christian images of God, the relationship with Jesus Christ, the sacramental imagination and a more authentic non-dualistic understanding of God. She emphasises that Catholic education should disturb our cosy images of God and sow the seeds of a more mature faith that opens the way to a lived faith in adulthood.

Orla Walsh writes as a parent. She speaks of the overwhelming responsibility she and her husband feel given that they accept they are the primary educators of their children. But school remains a critically important environment for the development of children. She cites valuable research with findings to support her claim that the Catholic school is of immense value to young children and teenagers.

John-Paul Sheridan writes from the perspective of a Diocesan Advisor for religious education. This role involves supporting schools and teachers in delivering and improving the programme in religious education. He describes visiting a large number of schools and reflects on how children grow in faith during their years in primary school.

Anne Hession asks the important questions, 'What in your life do you wish could continue into the next generation? What living have you found to be true and worthwhile?' Children who attend a Catholic school will be invited to *be* and to *live* in a certain way. She details the spirituality or philosophy of life proposed by the Catholic school.

These six articles provide key insights on the experience of Catholic schooling for children at the beginning of a new millennium.

Conclusion

Jesus revealed much about the reign of God through the parables that he told. Amongst the most important are those that speak of a sower sowing seed. Some seeds fell in thorns and were choked. Some fell in a drain and were drowned. Some fell in shallow earth and perished. And some fell in rich soil and yielded thirty, sixty, even a hundred fold. People often read these parables in a moralistic way – making judgments about the quality of people. But the true meaning of these parables is that the Word of God will not be frustrated by anything human – that though many seeds will not bear fruit, the true seed of the Word of God will bear a rich harvest in unexpected ways in our personal lives, in our families, in our communities, in our society, and, yes, in our schools. The task of Christian life is not to bemoan all that is wrong with us and our lives but to have the eyes to see that even in the midst of a sad and difficult world the seed of God's Word is bearing fruit in ways that we could never have imagined. Why send your child to a Catholic school? Because the seed of God's word will be sown in his/her heart. Who knows what rich harvest it might bear.

The Goals of Education and the Catholic School in Context

Donal McKeown

Education – Why Do We Have Schools?

When speaking to children at their Confirmation ceremony, I sometimes begin by asking them what their dreams are, now that they are leaving primary school. Such a question is guaranteed to get some creative responses: from having a good job to being a superhero, from having a ski lodge in the Alps to being a pop star. One child even announced that he wanted to be a spy. So many children have wonderfully fertile imaginations at ten. They are old enough to be surprisingly aware of many of life's possibilities, but young enough to maintain outrageous dreams. How we work with that creative energy lies at the heart of how we prepare our children to live and thrive in the midst of all the opportunities and challenges that life will throw at them.

Children don't learn in a vacuum. What parents know and experience plays a major role in how their children grow and develop. Every parent has dreams for their child. Those aspirations generally have to do with happiness and some degree of what is perceived as success in the various aspects of human life – work, status and relationships. Parents and family can obtain great satisfaction and joy from what their children achieve. And a parent's own sense of self-respect can have an impact on what their child attains – or fails to attain. Inevitably, parents who have experienced heartbreak and major disappointment in their own lives will influence what their children should expect. So it is not surprising that people in every society have tried to clarify what they understand by how we try to educate and prepare young people to make the best of the opportunities and challenges the world offers.

The ancient Greek philosophers believed that education was the search for the truth (Socrates), virtue (Aristotle) or the good (Plato). That is easy to say, but what is perceived as true, virtuous or good has changed in many ways. In twenty-first-century Ireland, as in much of western society, there is little left of the earlier consensus about the meaning of these deceptively simple words. Indeed, predominant postmodernist thought would suggest that, since there is no source outside us to define truth, virtue and good, those concepts mean whatever we believe them to be at a particular time.

This approach makes it much more difficult for increasingly secular societies to agree on what the goals, methods and content of education should be. It is always easier to value what we can measure rather than trying to measure what we value. Thus, it is not surprising that while educationalists will often espouse lofty words about the holistic development of the whole person, there is a temptation to reduce education to the non-contentious area of what is done in schools – that is, the accumulation of qualifications or training for jobs. If education is increasingly reduced to passing on useful skills in this way, it would explain why the idea of Catholic education is viewed with great suspicion by some.

Where there is uncertainty about what outcomes society really values, examination data can become a priority. Indeed, current government policies tend to prioritise the learning of what we can empirically prove and leave other imponderables to the realm of personal belief. So it would actually be strange if educational leaders were expected to aspire to any goals other than those which are SMART: specific, measurable, attainable, realistic and timely.

Even under the heading of measurable targets, schools are encouraged to emphasise certain statistics. Schools are rightly proud of how many of their past pupils have obtained places in the most prestigious universities or have senior places in society; however, they are not asked to produce data on how many young people do not blossom within their educational experience. This latter statistic might be just as revealing about what a school is achieving, or failing to achieve, for its young people.

Thus, much of the public discourse on the role and structure of education focuses on competition between schools to 'drive up standards', on educational league tables and on the delivery of a clearly identified curriculum content. Increasing use is made of the language of business and management, where parents are regarded as customers (to be persuaded to choose one school rather than another), pupils as consumers and schools as businesses which have to deliver a product. The status and desirability of a school risk being assessed primarily in terms of an audit that focuses on effectiveness, efficiency and value for money.[1]

In the context of such language, some schools are seen as more desirable because they facilitate access to high examination outcomes and companionship with other talented and upwardly mobile young people. It is not surprising that access to the 'best schools'

---

1   The 2010 Business Plan for the Northern Ireland Department of Education proposes for itself the following vision: 'DE exists to ensure that every learner fulfils her or his full potential at each stage of development' (www.deni.gov.uk/de_business_plan_2010_-11_english_pdf_version.pdf/). The Republic's Department of Education and Skills states that its mission is 'to provide high-quality education, which will enable individuals to achieve their full potential and to participate fully as members of society; and contribute to Ireland's social, cultural and economic development' (www.education.ie).

has become a hotly contested area. If education-as-qualifications is in short supply and a key asset in the race to the top, then parents will do everything to secure advantage for their own children. If the focus is, at least subliminally, on the measurable outcomes of income and social status, then education becomes a competitive rather than a collaborative world. This *context* of education becomes part of the *content*, its hidden curriculum.

There are, of course, those who oppose this reification of education, what Paulo Freire called 'the "banking" concept'.[2] Such authors see this as a cheapening of education, taking it away from any sense of human liberation and reducing it to a commodity to be traded and acquired by those with power. These authors are very critical of the fact that we have come a long way from prioritising truth, goodness and virtue.

What Do We Agree On?

In the absence of any social consensus about the meaning of education, what core elements might be essential if we wish to construct a model of education capable of responding to the growing needs of individuals and of society?

Education is more than the passing on of information

'Teachers don't teach subjects. They teach people'[3]

School examinations cannot hope to evaluate much more than how well pupils have learnt facts and skills. Most of that content may be valuable, enabling individuals to be literate, numerate, able to engage with the world in which we live and capable of making useful contributions to the quest for knowledge. But as well as having

---

2   Paulo Freire, *Pedagogy of the Oppressed: 30th Anniversary Edition* (New York: Continuum, 2000), p. 71.

3   Ken Dryden, *In School: Our Kids, Our Teachers, Our Classrooms* (Toronto: McClelland & Stewart, 1995), p. 4.

an informative value, education also plays an important formative role. Young people are not just being prepared for their future as citizens. They are already members of society. What they learn in the microcosm of the school community can be crucial when it comes to their contribution to the macrocosm of the adult world. How they experience the world they live in now will influence how they see the world that they will occupy in the future.

Thus, if we see education through this lens, good educators are not just those who clearly communicate the subject content of a course but those who use the context of acquiring information as a place where students will learn self-confidence, skills in working with other people, the ability to communicate, an openness to accepting responsibility for self and for others, and an ability to see the world through the eyes of others.

The atmosphere of a school – its ethos – is very hard to describe or analyse. But it can oppress and depress – or liberate and enthuse – the pupils, staff and parents. It is that ethos which nourishes the heart and not just the head of young learners. A good school energises staff to look after pupils in a way that goes far beyond the imparting of information which can be assessed in exams.

Humans learn as social beings

An elderly lady in rural Ireland was asked what it is like to be 100. 'Well,' she said, 'there is not much peer pressure!'

No one lives or grows up in a vacuum. School is not the only or the primary context in which young people learn. Even the child in the womb has absorbed much before birth. Attitudes to self and to others are heavily influenced by childhood experiences. While there is much argument over the relationship between nature and nurture, what a child experiences as 'home' is the environment where much is learned about nutrition, dress, interaction between men and women, and self-confidence. Children do not just learn about things from others; their sense of personal identity is heavily influenced by how they believe others see them. Learning is a social rather than a solitary process.

Of course, schools do not exist in a vacuum either. Societies and communities have values and assumptions that justify how people have got to where they are, individually and communally. All teaching and learning about science, history, literature and geography takes place within a set of cultural assumptions about what is valued in the community. Parents will generally wish that their children attend schools that support their own convictions, and international legal instruments specifically allow for the rights of parents in that regard.

Schools are therefore vehicles for the socialisation of children. That process is facilitated when there is consistency between the intellectual development offered and the emotional and moral growth fostered (or not fostered, as the case may be). It is facile to imagine that the effects of education can be measured on the basis of how well young people are prepared for answering examination questions.

Human learning is shaped by the quality of human relationships

'Pupils don't consciously remember what teachers taught them. They often don't even remember what teachers did or said. But they never forget how teachers made them feel.' (Anon)

If we learn in the context of human relationships, then we grow or are damaged through the quality of these relationships. That does not merely apply to learning about how we relate to others. Because we develop in a dialectical process, our relationship with ourselves is dependent to a large extent on how we perceive other's perception of us. A sense of being loved, of being bad, of feeling secure or being nagged by an inferiority complex – all of these are affected through our key relationships in life.

Young people spend an average of 15,000 hours in secondary school,[4] comprising a much greater part of their waking days than they spend with their parents and families. Teachers can inspire love of a subject or confidence in one's own abilities to achieve. In adulthood, people look back on their school days with very different memories. These recollections can be very clear. For some, school was a place where they felt crushed by harshness or fear, or by the sheer boredom of time apparently wasted; they look back in anger and with regret at opportunities lost. For others, it was a place where they felt accepted, encouraged or trusted, an environment where they discovered liberation in learning or in creativity.

This does not imply that a good school is a place where everybody is 'nice' to everyone else. Many people are inspired by teachers who are demanding and challenging, just as many teachers have the highest regard for leaders who take them much further as professionals than they thought they could or would want to go. As with all relationships, adults and children appear to be most at ease with consistency and dependability in how they are treated.

Every individual has a rich world of the imagination

'Imagination is the eye of the soul' (Joseph Joubert)
One of the great human realities is that we have a rich imagination. That does not merely refer to daydreaming, wishful thinking or childish fairy stories. Human maturation involves being in touch with that inner world where creativity is born and where our hidden selves find expression through images, music, art and movement. We need only reflect on the power of flags, colours, songs and smells to evoke emotion. That power has often been harnessed for good and for less laudable purposes.

4 Michael Rutter et al., *Fifteen Thousand Hours: Secondary Schools and Their Effects On Children* (London: Open Books, 1979).

Dreams can be mirrors of that rich symbolic world, but the imagination is not just part of the way in which humans process memory and experience. That hidden world also influences how individuals and communities interpret what we experience. It provides the interpretative assumptions with which we give shape and meaning to life and to our place in the world. It would be a tragedy if educators neglected the non-empirical world of creativity, symbols, values and the arts. It would be a poor education that failed to develop pupils' ability to engage with, and speak of, their inner world.

Education and culture

'Culture is like an ocean, surrounding us as water a fish, the air we breathe.' (Michael Paul Gallagher)

People in Ireland – and many abroad – have some idea of what characterises 'Irish' culture. We may think about music, dance, sport and other things that make us who we are and which distinguish the Irish from, for example, the Russians or the people of the Andes. But culture is much more than activities that people can take part in.

The word 'culture' is also used to describe what a group of people take to be the normal thing to do. Human beings want to have a sense of belonging and acceptance, so it is helpful and nourishing to conform to what significant others see to be the standards. That applies to dress, looks, accepted symbols of success, attitudes and behaviour. We have only to look at photographs of ourselves going back over the last decades to know just how each generation and each group has developed its own standards of what is normal and desirable. The beautiful car, the 'cool' clothes and the popular music of earlier decades may well seem out of place, indeed embarrassing, in the twenty-first century. Each generation develops its own distinct identity, partly based on received standards but at least partially in rebellion to that prized by their parents.

This cultural environment provides the context in which all learning takes place. It is an asset in that individuals can have much in common and can understand the significance of words, festivities and achievements. It can be a disadvantage when it limits the individual's ability to think outside the parameters of cultural assumptions. It can be used as a firm foundation on which to build. It can be used as a prison in which to limit people so that they accept what the cultural gatekeepers want them to believe. We have ample examples of that in totalitarian regimes such as Nazi Germany and communist countries. In these countries, ordinary, decent people came to do terrible things because the culture told them that they were the right thing to do.

The imagination plays a key role in the formation of each person. This comes through culture, slogans, subliminal influences, advertising, music and experience. We can ask whether it is possible to build a culture that nourishes a young person's ability to experience life in a rich way and communicate that experience in a healthy manner. Father Michael Paul Gallagher suggests that culture is not merely a sociological phenomenon, something essentially on the surface of how we experience life. He believes that 'culture provides environments for choice and cultural change alters the frontiers of what is imaginable'.[5]

Some will suggest that any excessive parental, social or church influence is not education but indoctrination, trapping the child and limiting their freedom, now and in the future. However, the question for parents is not whether they should seek to influence their children's formation, but what influences and cultural assumptions will help to mould the growing mind if they do not take responsibility for how the impressionable young person develops. The 'hidden persuaders' of popular culture are happy to exploit new customers

5   Michael Paul Gallagher, 'Imagination Gone Secular', *The Furrow* 57 (November 2006): p. 592.

for commercial reasons. The world of advertising uses profound psychological insights in order to influence young consumers in their purchases and in their aspirations. There is no neutral environment for the development of the human imagination.

Part of any culture is the story that its members tell about themselves. Narratives are a key way in which we both order our experience and can engage with that of another person. Thus every individual has a story to tell about how they came to this particular time in their life. Similarly, racial and social groups have a way of interpreting their history. The celebrations that mark either the nationalist or unionist communities in Ireland are examples of how powerful cultural narratives can be.

Such narratives influence how communal and individual experiences are processed. After all, the story we tell about ourselves – individually and communally – is not just made up of objectively correct words about what happened in the past, but is partly an explanation of 'who I am today'. It is the narrative that joins the various dots and gives some meaning to the scattered events of our lives. It provides a filter for what stories we want to hear. We all listen and read selectively. Individuals and groups can feel very threatened in the depths of their being when their story is contradicted. The particular way of describing who we are and how we got here provides the context for learning.

The story about the Catholic Church that I grew up with was based on a clear and inspiring narrative. The Church stood for truth (thus it was persecuted in Eastern European countries), for missionary work (the thousands of Irish nuns, brothers, priests and lay people in developing countries) and for building communities of faith and goodness around the country. It was a story of inexorable growth for the true Church. But that story also made it hard to believe stories which suggested that some people in the Church were motivated by anything other than gospel values and idealism. If our 'story' were true, it couldn't be true that there was sexual abuse and domestic violence in good Irish Catholic families, parishes or religious institutions. It most certainly couldn't be true that some priests and religious were taking advantage of children in brutal ways. That would contradict the story on which I had based so much. It was an 'appalling vista'. The story that inspired us also limited us. Like any convenient story that we like to tell ourselves, it was a partial truth fossilised into heresy.

I have suggested that the cultural environment in which we live plays an influential role in how we see and talk about our world. But anthropologist Mary Douglas has gone deeper. She has argued very cogently that the rigidity or looseness of our social structures determines whether we see symbolic gestures and vocabulary as meaningful. Our social environment affects not only the content of our narratives but our ability to create shared language codes with which to articulate our stories.[6] How our society is structured has an enormous influence on our perception of the value of places, objects, rituals, sporting colours and symbols. Thus, tightly knit groups – like much of Ireland a couple of generations ago – instinctively find powerful importance in practices like fasting, religious observance and 'good manners'. They also find it easier to hand on their values to the next generation through these potent bearers of agreed meaning. Societies with a much weaker sense of internal bonds and external borders – like most western societies – perceive little value in such symbolic language and gestures. Meaning becomes individualised or of value only in specific sub-cultures. The problem for these later social constructs is that there is no shared language code with which to communicate meaning and engage with the imagination. An individualised society risks fragmentation unless it can find some other social 'glue'.

---

6 Mary Douglas, *Purity and Danger: An Analysis of Pollution and Taboo* (London: Routledge and Kegan Paul, 1966); Mary Douglas, *Natural Symbols: Explorations in Cosmology* (London: Barrie and Jenkins, 1973).

Many people will seek to justify certain social structures as better or less beneficial and champion definitive labels such as 'progressive', 'liberal', 'traditional' and 'conservative'. However, the empirical sciences show that there are advantages and disadvantages in each particular type of society. Thus, Ireland knows the strengths and weaknesses of the traditional sorts of community that predominated until the final quarter of the twentieth century. Similarly, many know the opportunities and dangers that inhere in the current, rapidly changing social structures and mores.

Therefore, the educational experience is heavily influenced by the 'informal' or 'hidden' curricula of a school. Its story about itself – how the community is structured, the semiotics and imagery, what is celebrated and prioritised – all can play an important role in developing or impairing a child. Quality education wishes to inspire and promote. It wants to avoid what William Wordsworth meant when he said that 'Shades of the prison-house begin to close/ Upon the growing boy.'[7]

How Does Catholic Education Measure Up?

In many western countries Catholic education was often assumed to be the normal form of education for Catholics. In these societies religious identity was taken, until recently, to be something that a person was born with. Thus, despite modest levels of church attendance there is still ample reference in Northern Ireland to 'Catholic' areas and 'Protestant' marches. Educational choices were dominated by loyalty to the religious identity a child was allocated. In many cases, Catholic schools assumed that one of their tasks was to keep children Catholic by handing on the various elements of that identity – including the culture in which local Catholicism was growing. One of the results was that the promotion of religio-cultural

---

7   William Wordsworth, 'Intimations of Immortality from Recollections of Early Childhood', v.

identity sometimes risked getting in the way of the biblical teaching that faith is a choice, not a fate. Another outcome has been that, in some countries, parents and parish communities have, in practice, 'sub-contracted' the religious formation of children to the parish school. The celebration of the key Sacraments of Initiation have increasingly been seen as school events taking place in the parish church.

When faced with challenges about the role of Catholic education in western societies, some have justifiably defended the right of Church communities to provide an educational curriculum that includes an explicit catechetical content. Indeed, the right of faith communities to provide – and of parents to have – a system of education which reflects their philosophical and religious convictions is firmly established in international instruments of human rights. The European Convention on Human Rights, Protocol 1 (1951) Article 2, for example, states that

> in the exercise of any functions which it assumes in relation to education and teaching, the state shall respect the right of parents to ensure such education and teaching as is in conformity with their own religious and philosophical convictions.

The United Nations International Covenant on Economic, Social and Cultural Rights (1966) Article 13 (3) upholds

> the liberty of parents ... to choose for their children schools ... which conform to such minimum educational standards as may be laid down or approved by the state and to ensure the religious and moral education of their children in conformity with their own convictions.

This in turn confirms the fundamental principle enunciated in the Universal Declaration on Human Rights (1948) Article 26 (3) that 'Parents shall have a prior right to choose the kind of education that shall be given to their children.'

However, there are some dangers inherent in espousing only this justification for Catholic education. This line of argument risks suggesting that Catholic education is essentially just a good form of secular education with time set aside for religious education. Alternatively, it may be portrayed as an attempt by Catholics to set themselves apart from the rest of society.

Yet, at the heart of the Church's understanding of Catholic education is the conviction that Catholic schools are based on a particular philosophy of education as well as having a specific educational curriculum. At heart, Catholic education claims to be different because it offers a particular *content* of education and a specific *context* for education. Thus the core justification for Catholic education will include the right of parents to send their children to schools where they can develop in their understanding of Catholicism. But it will also include the conviction that there is room for different philosophies of education in the public education sphere. The former justification may be questioned by those who ask whether public monies should be spent on denominational education. The latter argument asserts the right of Catholics (and others) to access a particular form of educational experience, especially when it is both very effective and efficient.

Since the Second Vatican Council, there has been a series of documents on the Catholic understanding of Catholic education.[8]

---

8 *Gravissimum Educationis* (1965), *The Catholic School* (1977), *Lay Catholics in Schools: Witnesses to Faith* (1982), *The Religious Dimension of Education in a Catholic School* (1988), *The Catholic School on the Threshold of the Third Millennium* (1997), *Consecrated Persons and their Mission in Schools* (2002), *Educating Together in Catholic Schools*, (2007). Available at www.vatican.va. In the rest of this essay, references to these documents will be given using the year of publication and the paragraph number.

The Catholic school is part of the Church's mission in Christ's name

These Vatican documents clearly situate the Catholic school in the context of the Church's overall mission: 'The mission of the Church is to evangelise' (1988, n. 66). The Church has one mission – that is to 'go and make disciples of all nations' (Mt 28:19). All Church activity is focused on this outcome. If Jesus came to proclaim the reign of God, and if the Church is called to be 'a kind of sacrament or sign of intimate union with God, and of the unity of all humankind' (*Lumen Gentium*, n. 1), then anything that bears the name of Christian or Catholic cannot but have that as its goal. Thus there is an insistence that 'the Catholic school finds its justification in the mission of the Church' (1988, n. 34). It is clearly stated that 'the Catholic school participates in the evangelising mission of the Church and is the privileged environment in which Christian education is carried out' (1997, n. 11). That situates our schools not just in the sense of their having to work within the local Christian community, but also in the belief that a Catholic school 'fully enters into the salvific mission of the Church' (1982, n. 38). Indeed, schools are described as being established precisely because 'they are a privileged means of promoting the formation of the whole person' (1977, n. 8).

Catholic education is a community-based process of formation

All education takes place in a much broader context than just that of the school. As far as Catholic education is concerned, all the documents are very aware that the three-legged stool of family, community and school is the ideal context for providing support. Thus, the Catholic school cannot be separated from those factors outside school, which contribute to a rounded faith development of young people. The community, which includes 'students, parents, teachers, non-teaching personnel and the school management',

> can create an environment for living, in which the values are mediated by authentic interpersonal relations between the various members of which it is composed. Its highest aim is the complete and comprehensive education of the person. (2002, n. 41)

After all, the young people of today are not just the adults of tomorrow, but people who must learn today many of the things they will need tomorrow. Schools are not merely exam factories but living communities and are 'considered as microcosms in which oases are created where the bases are laid for living responsibly in the macrocosm of society' (2002, n. 43).

Unless our schools and their associated parish communities can bear witness to a community of co-responsible relationships then we may clearly see the lean, efficient, effective secularist educational trees but miss the beauty of the forest. If we prepare our pupils mainly to do well in a purely competitive society, we cease to be sources of Christ's healing.

Catholic schools are a key place where the Church is encountered

Because of the ecclesial identity of the Catholic school (1997, n. 11), the pupil, teacher and parent experience of such a school is essentially an ecclesial experience. The whole is incarnated in the specific. For many young people who are Catholic, and for others who do not belong to that community, what they see in school will make tangible what the Catholic community is. In coming to understand what the Church is, the experience that people have of a school is itself an education. The 1982 document says that the 'educational community of a school is itself a school' (1982, n. 22), for learning is a social experience rather than a solitary one.

Thus, a school that is precious about itself communicates much about the insignificant value of relationships with others outside the invisible walls of the school community. There is the ever-present temptation for a successful Catholic school to promote priorities and policies that support its particular place in the secular pecking order, with little sense of the effects these might have on other Catholic schools, or the model of Christian faith that it communicates. A very different message about the mission and identity of the Church is communicated by a school that is clearly part of the Church and its mission and which acts in solidarity with others within the Catholic family of schools.

Therefore, a Catholic school needs to do more than just create a cosy atmosphere of Christian community. Unless it is part of a wider community of all ages, unless it is part of a missionary Church, then it is not universal – Catholic. For this reason, 'the school fulfils its vocation to be a genuine experience of Church only if it takes its stand within the organic pastoral work of the Christian community' (1997, n. 12). That coordination and integration needs a lot of work if the school is to be a local example of 'a kind of sacrament or sign of intimate union with God, and of the unity of all humankind' (*Lumen Gentium*, n. 1). That does not mean control and conformity. In fact one of the strengths of the Catholic tradition has been the great range of specific vocations and spiritualities that exist within the one family. The task is to encourage that diversity, within the one mission of the Church to proclaim the Good News by word and deed, to be a sign of the possibility of unity in diversity in a very fragmented and varied world. But it does imply that the range of traditions and charisms needs to be located in a cohesive rather than a competing provision.

Catholic education seeks to form the whole person

Christian theology is based on Emmanuel, God with us, and the Vatican's documents make it clear that this evangelisation is not directed just at the head, or at some separated spiritual side of people. The purpose of evangelisation is 'the interior transformation and the renewal of humanity' (1988, n. 66), 'the promotion of total human formation' (1988, n. 31). That is what is involved in renewing the face of the earth. That is what is involved in proclaiming that the 'Word became flesh and lived among us' (Jn 1:14). The Catholic educational experience thus involves an integration of *information* and *formation*, leading to fundamental *transformation*.

It involves integrating faith, culture and life (1988, nn. 31–4). It is about a process of individual and communal maturation, 'life long learning' in the context of faith, based on constant renewal through grace of our vision and of our ability to see, and that can take place only in the context of a community, of a pilgrim people. The Council document talks about the creation of community permeated with gospel values (1965, n. 8). That is how the face of the earth is to be renewed. Our schools have to model this, not just in our schools but far beyond them.

Interface between faith and culture

Pope John Paul II was consistently clear about this integrated vision for a Christianity that penetrates to the heart of our society. That has been made abundantly clear in his document *Ecclesia in Europa*.[9] Here he committed the Church to being actively involved in creating a Europe that is not just a market that knows about prices, but a community that has values – a community aware of its past and that has retained a commitment to beauty and to truth. The role of education in the creation of this new European humanism is vital (EE, n. 60). Christianity has to be incarnated in various ways in different

---

9   *Ecclesia in Europa* (2003). Further references to the document will be given as EE, followed by the note number.

cultures, imbuing each with a gospel perspective, taking the best from each and enriching it with the vision of the Creator. Thus the 1988 document is clear that '[o]ne of the characteristics of a Catholic school is that it interpret and give order to human culture in the light of faith' (1988, n. 52).

In an educational world, which increasingly focuses on discreet subjects and accumulated qualifications, it is this integrated perspective on learning that is one of the great strengths of the Catholic vision of education. The complementary roles of school teaching and community catechesis involve an integrated ecclesial approach to faith formation. It has already been mentioned that two of the documents considered here are clear that, as well as looking at an integration of faith and culture and of faith and life, we are also looking at an integration of faith and science/reason. This is because the Church, in all that we do, are seeking to communicate 'an organic presentation of Christian anthropology' (1988, n. 56) and trying to overcome some of the problems of a fragmented and insufficient curriculum (1988, n. 55).

There is a Catholic worldview

As such, the Catholic school becomes not so much a school that gives a good secular education to Catholics, but rather 'a centre in which a specific concept of the world, of people and of history is developed and conveyed' (1977, n. 8). The 1982 document also uses a phrase taken from Pope Paul VI and found in much of his writings: the education in the Catholic school is not just directed to convincing people of the goodness of the gospel, '[t]he Catholic educator … must be committed to the task of forming men and women who will make the "civilisation of love" a reality' (1982, n. 19).[10]

---

10 There is interesting material on the Catholic worldview in, for example, Thomas Groome, *What Makes Us Catholic: Eight Gifts For Life* (San Francisco: Harper, 2002) and Andrew Greeley, *The Catholic Imagination* (Berkley, Los Angeles: University of California Press, 2000).

And that is why the Catholic school is much more than just a place for teaching catechetics. Of course, religious instruction is a key element in the formal curriculum. That element has to be taken very seriously and taught by people who have a passion for and commitment to their subject. 'The special character of the Catholic school ... is precisely the quality of the religious instruction integrated into the overall education of the students' (1988, n. 66). However that 1988 document remains clear that catechesis (the aim of which is maturity) happens most especially in the local Christian community (1988, n. 69). The school offers its unique contribution but cannot do the whole job. Schools aim at communicating knowledge. Thus 'religious instruction and catechesis are at the same time distinct and complementary' (1988, n. 70). Yet again, it is apparent that the work of the community and the work of the school should seek to work towards the same goal. A freelance school cannot really call itself Catholic.

The School – Part of a Church of Mission and Service

The school, then, if it is to be Catholic, has to be reaching into the heart of its own community, contributing to that community's growth and development. But what constitutes its community? If we are to engage in the transformation through the grace of Jesus, then the Catholic school has to reach out beyond its natural cosy constituency. The confidence born of identity leads to the ability to engage, rather than to be protective. That engagement will involve dialogue with the secular world in all its aspects – law, medicine, politics, human rights, justice issues, the developing world. Education, then, is about giving people the vocabulary to engage with these core issues, to be unhappy with the right questions rather than simply being happy with the wrong answers. It will mean working with those who are best able to influence the world at that level of society. Yet that inclusiveness also means, as the 1997 document makes clear, being a school that is there especially for the weakest in society (1997, n. 15). After all, education is not given for the purpose of gaining power, but as an aid towards a fuller understanding of, and communion with people, events and things. Knowledge is not to be considered as a means of material prosperity and success, but as a call to serve and to be responsible for others. (1977, n. 56)

This has practical implications if our schools are to bear witness to gospel values. Joseph O'Keefe's famous slogan 'no margin, no mission' was very critical of Catholic schools in the US that were happy to stay in prosperous areas where there were margins on which to survive, but that tended to withdraw their mission from the poorer areas.[11] Our schools would be doing an injustice to the spirit of many of their founders – and would themselves be profoundly impoverished – if they were to forget where, when and why their congregations were founded.

There is no shortage of the new poor in our society. Poverty is always a relative rather than an absolute term. Research has suggested that it is this relative poverty that kills the human spirit just as starvation kills the body. Again the gospel call to work for the breaking down of barriers between and within communities is at the heart of the ecclesial mission of all our schools. Indeed, part of that ecclesial witness means that, first and foremost, 'the Church offers its educational service to the poor or those who are deprived of family help or those who are far from the faith' (1977, n. 58, quoting GE, n. 9).

The Catholic school is thus concerned with the transmission of values lived out in a community context. Indeed the documents recognise the temptation for a Catholic school to replicate not the gospel's idea of a community but rather the competitiveness and individualism that are widespread in our society. The 1977 document goes as far as saying that the school is called to 'render a humble

---

11 Terence H. McLaughlin, Joseph O'Keefe and Bernadette O'Keefe, eds, *The Contemporary Catholic School: Context, Identity and Diversity* (London: Falmer Press, 1996).

loving service to the Church by ensuring that she is present in the scholastic world for the benefit of the human family' (1977, n. 62). Thus, the individual school has its unique role to play, but that role only has meaning if it serves both the mission of the Church and the salvation of the world.

Unity and Diversity

This is of course based not just on Church documents but on scriptural insights. If we want to check our charter documents, the New Testament is full of examples of Jesus – and later the early Church – constantly seeking to build integration and overcome exclusion. The Samaritan woman (Jn 4) was not just a woman from Samaria. For the Jews, she was a member of a race to be shunned for all sorts of watertight theological and social reasons. And within her own Samaritan people, she was excluded because of her sexual track record. Otherwise she wouldn't have been coming to the well at the hottest part of the day. Similarly, many of the sick, whom Jesus healed, were not just physically made well again – lepers, disabled, blind were then included in their society. That meant gaining a new understanding of themselves in relationship to their own self-image, to other people's view of them and their relationship with God. The kingdom of God was to be inclusive rather than exclusive.

The word 'church' occurs only twice in all the gospels. But on many occasions Jesus says to the disciples, 'You are …', using an image rather than an abstract definition of what members of the Church are called to be. The authors of the New Testament letters similarly use a whole range of images to describe the mystery of the Church – many of these images are clearly about us as together rather than as isolated individuals.[12] They include

---

12 For an interesting look at these images, see Hans-Ruedi Weber, *Experiments with Bible Study* (Geneva: World Council of Churches, 1983), pp. 225–32.

» Sheep of Christ (Jn 10)
» Branches of the vine (Jn 15)
» Christ's body (1 Cor 12:27)
» Ambassadors for Christ (2 Cor 5:20)
» The household of God (Eph 2:19)
» Living stones (1 Pt 2:5)

Again, belonging and interconnectedness appear to be at the core of the New Testament vision for God's people. But the New Testament also includes another emphasis, which touches on this. While all are members of the Body of Christ, there is a great variety of gifts (Eph 4:7; 1 Cor 12:4-31). When writing to the church in Corinth, Paul has to take a very strong line against those who think that their particular gifts must take priority over those of others.

The challenge for the Church is not to search for conformity, but to develop the potential of the God-given diversity of gifts and graces that we have with the Body of Christ. The search for a unity in diversity is the real struggle that we have to face in building community. How can we enhance the status and dignity of the individual through the structures of belonging that we put in place in the service of the kingdom? That is the ideal that we try to embody in our educational provision. How do we provide equality of dignity and of belonging while responding to the huge range of needs that different people have? That is a real practical problem rather than just a theological conundrum, and it will affect just what model of Church we communicate.

Conclusion

The Catholic worldview includes a commitment not to separate itself from the world but, like Jesus, to immerse itself in the reality of human life. Thus, Catholic education has adapted to different environments down through history. But at its heart has always been the conviction that the search for truth and the use of reason can only serve both the search for the one who is the Way, the Truth and the Life, and the humanisation of the world. Faith and reason are companions, not enemies.

In a rapidly changing world, Catholic education is faced with the need to reinvent itself for new environments. However, the many strengths of the Catholic school will continue to give encouragement to those who must lead that development.

First, we have a treasure trove of visionary documents that offer an inspirational view of education and a hope-filled message for our young people. Second, all the evidence shows that Catholic schools are popular, not despite the fact that they are explicitly faith based, but precisely because the faith identity is at the heart of what inspires commitment to a different way of being. It does not merely offer secular education with a little religion on the side. It offers a way of looking at the world that emphasises community, reason, high expectations and a belief in a God who believes in people. Catholic education will be able to promote its contribution to the common good only to the extent that it is Catholic and different in its structures, message and way of acting. Catholic schools will be more true to their identity when they measure what they value and don't just value what they can measure. Third, we have a shared commitment to Catholic education within a varied range of traditions and spiritualities.

All of these attributes share the Catholic genius, which seeks to balance subsidiarity and local decision making with solidarity and a sense of co-responsibility with others.

We will have gone some distance down the right road when our schools have moved beyond merely offering education for ethnic Catholics and can confidently offer Catholic education to all who wish to avail of it. If we can help young people to articulate their dreams in the context of a God who never loses his dream for us

– individually and communally – we will have become a source of hope. And we will have become more like the missionary Church that Pope Francis has invited us to be.

Catholic Education as Lived Experience of Faith

Nuala O'Loan

Many factors will influence the school you send your child to, some of them entirely pragmatic. There may be only one school in the area in which you live, and transport to any other school may be unavailable. There may be many schools in the general area, but you may not have a car and there may be no buses, and therefore whilst theoretically there is choice, the prospect of a two- or three-mile walk twice a day to and from school, in all weathers, possibly pushing a baby's buggy and holding onto the hand of a toddler, will dictate that the child must go to the nearest school. I have vivid memories of such a walk during a period of my own life: the time spent preparing three children for the outdoors, getting them safely there and back again, dealing with all the wet coats and hats and gloves, and trying to avoid the cars which drove blithely through huge puddles. Or, alternatively, coping with the hot and fractious child who was walking beside the buggy and wanted to rest rather than walk, meant that it was a demanding exercise just to get one child to school. For others, however, there will be choice and the decision which is made will probably have a fundamental impact on the rest of the child's life. The ethos and values of the school and of those who attend it will be profoundly formative. Parents are aware of this and they very often agonise over which school will be best for their child.

The availability of faith schools is something which we enjoy now in many countries, but which cannot be taken for granted in an increasingly secular society. There are those who argue that religion no longer has relevance in the modern world. Yet the huge number of people gathered at the Vatican, thousands of whom were very young, on the recent election of Pope Francis would indicate otherwise. What was in some ways even more interesting, and indeed more unexpected, was the huge number of journalists who gathered to report the conclave and the inauguration. At least 6,000 were accredited. Similarly, the spectacular success of the 2013 World Youth Day in Brazil, when over three million young people gathered on Copacabana Beach, demonstrated the passionate enthusiasm and joy that many continue to experience in the celebration of their faith.

Sitting in the House of Lords, I have heard Catholic social teaching cited in the cause of the poor, the marginalised and the lost on a number of occasions – not by Catholics but by other Christians. Indeed the Archbishop of Canterbury, Justin Welby, is greatly influenced by Catholic social teaching. In the 2011 census 84.2 per cent of the Irish population declared themselves to be Catholic, some 3,861,300 people – a surprising figure in a country sometimes proclaimed as being 'post-Catholic'. Only 277,237 people declared themselves as having 'no religion'.

Yet rates of regular traditional practice of religion are undoubtedly falling. Across Ireland the change is marked, with rapidly diminishing congregations in many churches. There can be no doubt that people are now making decisions about how they live their lives which were not made by their parents and grandparents. Changing social mores mean that Ireland, north and south, is a very different country than it once was. Catholic practice, whatever that means, has changed. However, the fact that people do not go to church regularly does not appear to indicate that they do not see themselves as Catholic, or do not wish to send their children to Catholic schools. Indeed, they are still doing so in huge numbers. Moreover, when presented with the possibility of a change in the way in which education is delivered – a change that would result in schools being separated from the Church – parents articulate very little enthusiasm in its favour. At the present time there are extensive opportunities in Ireland to send a child to a Catholic school: Catholic primary and secondary education remains the norm in Ireland and is freely available throughout Northern Ireland.

Of course many schools will be capable of providing high-quality education in acceptable facilities. The reason parents may make the decision to send their children to a Catholic school is that it is a place founded in faith – faith that matters. A Catholic school must be a place in which faith is enabled, encouraged, modelled, facilitated and taught. It must be absolutely central to the school, not just provided for in timetabled religious education classes. The compelling reason to send your child to a Catholic school is that you want them to learn about and grow in faith. A Catholic school is entitled to start from a religious perspective, and to teach children in a way that will give them not just knowledge but a lifelong understanding of the need to ask questions and to search for truth and wisdom. Yet Catholic schools are not exclusive, rather they are inclusive and teach tolerance and respect for others and for diversity.

As Catholics we believe that we are on a journey in faith: that God made us; that he has a plan for each of us, as Cardinal Newman said; and that our lives here are to be lived in love for the God who made us, and in love for each other and the magnificent world in which we live. This is not a theoretical, vague love. Rather, living in love will inevitably take us to places to which we would rather not go, present us with challenges and demand that we give without limit as Christ gave himself for us. Catholicism, as Fr Robert Barron notes, is a form of life, a path that one walks. It is a way of seeing, a frame of mind, an attitude, but more than this, it is a manner of moving and acting, standing and relating. It is not simply a matter of the mind but of the body as well. In fact, one could say that Christianity is not real until it has insinuated itself into the blood and the bones, until it becomes an instinct, as much physical as spiritual. Perhaps, the most direct description is this: Christianity, the way of Jesus Christ, is a culture, a style of life supported by a unique set of convictions, assumptions, hopes, and practices.[1]

Catholic schools help develop the early teaching provided by parents about this way of life. None of us are perfect. In our human frailty none of us have the ability to live that calling to love which is part of being Catholic as we might wish to do. Indeed there will be those of us who will, like St Augustine, say, 'Lord make me holy but not just yet.' Catholic schools, if they are worthy of the name, will give children the experience of learning to live in love.

Pope Benedict XVI, speaking to pupils from Catholic schools across the United kingdom at St Mary's University College, said:

What God wants for each of you is that you should become holy. He loves you more than you could ever begin to imagine, and he wants the very best for you. And by far the best thing is to grow in holiness … I am asking you not to be content with second best. I am asking you not to pursue one limited goal and ignore all the others. Having money makes it possible to be generous and do good in the world, but on its own, it is not enough to make us happy. Being highly skilled in some activity or profession is good, but it will not satisfy us unless we aim for something greater still. It might make us famous. It will not

---

1   Fr Robert Barron, *The Strangest Way: Walking the Christian Path* (Maryknoll, NY: Orbis Books, 2002), p. 13.

make us happy. Happiness is something we all want, but one of the great tragedies of the world is that so many people never find it, because they look for it in the wrong places. The key is very simple. Happiness is to be found in God.[2]

Traditionally, schools have formed one part of a triangle for passing on the faith, alongside parents and parish. Primary schools have a special place in the community of the parish, which is part of the wider community of the Church. Secondary schools, often serving a larger area, can be the place where children learn not just maths and geography and all the other subjects of a modern curriculum, but also how to live as Catholics in the world today.

Faith is not just a matter of going to church on Sunday. If we act the words inherent in the final words of the Mass, 'Go and spread the gospel', then we each have responsibilities inherent in our faith. As parents, godparents, members of all the different communities to which we belong in the parish, in schools and in the wider world, we each have a role to play in nurturing our children and their future.

This means that parents have a legitimate right to expect certain things of Catholic schools, and of all those who work in them. Parents have the right to expect that their children will be nourished, cared for and educated, but above all that they will experience the love of God in everything they do, that they will learn about their faith, will be encouraged to see their fellow pupils and all the children of the world as God's children, their brothers and sisters in Christ, as part of a family and part of his mystical body.

There are few of us who, in the course of our lives, have not met truly good people — holy people whose lives are lived in and for Christ, informed by the presence of the Holy Spirit and who know that they are on the way home to the Father who made them. Their

---

2 Benedict XVI, 'Celebration of Catholic Education: Address of the Holy Father to Pupils', St Mary's University College, Twickenham (17 September 2010).

constant references to the things of God, to thanking him for good things, for happy moments, for those whom he sends into our lives, for the world in which we spend our lives; their prayer when things are difficult or when we face moments of grief and tragedy; their ability to live through the most difficult and challenging moments in faith, knowing that even when God seems not to be there, he really is there, and it is just that we cannot, for that moment, that time, hear his voice, mark them as people of God. Such people who have come into my path – and there have been many of them – have enriched my life, helped me to reach an understanding of what may seem inexplicable and given me the sense and the knowledge of the impact of God's grace on me. It was not just their kindness, their humanity, their goodness; it was their faith – so much more profound than goodness – which helped me to comprehend the presence of God in my life and helped me in the journey to know, love and serve him in all that I do and with all whom I meet. This is the essence of my existence.

These lived experiences of faith may be difficult concepts to articulate but they are the essence of relationship with God and give a whole different meaning to life. If a child is to grow in faith then they need as much exposure as possible to people who share that belief. Such opportunities can best be secured in a school dedicated to God, in which children learn every day about the fact that God loves them.

It is, unfortunately, the case that both parents and children have had experiences of Catholic schools very different from those that should be the standard. This does not mean that there is no purpose in sending a child into a Catholic school; rather it indicates that certain schools or individuals have failed in their responsibilities and obligations. Children and parents are acutely sensitive to the behaviour of those in authority or with responsibility in their school. They will see 'do as I say, not as I do' as an example of hypocrisy at best, and of an absence of lived faith at worst. We all know some of the past failings of Catholic educational institutions – sexual and physical abuse of children and the more common rudeness, contempt and derision with which pupils were treated. There can be no effective communication of faith where children are taught to love one another but do not themselves experience love.

Our schools are now acutely aware of these issues and much work goes on to ensure that children have an experience of school consistent with lived faith. Schools now articulate their ethos in their public documents that parents can examine, with an opportunity to approach the school about anything causing them concern. Parents are encouraged to become involved in school life, as parent governors, members of the Board of Management, as part of parent–teacher associations, by assisting in sacramental preparation, helping develop children's skills and accompanying them on school trips. All this allows parents to contribute to the development of the community life of the school and to give children a better understanding of the world for which they will have responsibility. For parents of children in the Catholic school system, such involvement is an opportunity to live their faith and to make a contribution to the whole school, not just to the interests of their own children.

Every life has its moments of difficulty, grief and tragedy. Every school has to deal in the course of the average year with some profoundly difficult situations. Children may be touched by death and serious illness, even suicide, whether of a parent or a sibling, or someone much loved in the wider family or community. They may have to deal with the consequences of unemployment, with poverty in all its forms, with bullying in school and outside it, with the consequences of drug and alcohol addiction, with loneliness and isolation. When these things happen, the child affected will have to cope whilst still trying to function within school. Not an easy task. Every school will attempt to look after its children at these times.

However, with an ethos predicated upon love of God and the love that God has for each little child, Catholic schools provide a special environment in which such children can work through their problems. Jesus' teachings 'I am with you always' and 'be not afraid' offer a sturdy backdrop.

Catholic schools are uniquely placed to ensure that there is a connectedness between the spirituality which the school seeks to promote and the daily life of the school; between life in school and the greater world around the children. Above all, they can help children to understand that the essence of Catholic spirituality for each of them is their individual relationship with God. Children will learn that best by being in the company of those who themselves believe in God and believe that he loves them and holds them in the palm of his hand, like the little old man who sat in a French church for long hours each day and who, when asked why he did so, is said to have replied, 'I am watching God watching me.' If children are in places where they meet those who truly believe, they will come to know that tenderness.

Children educated in Catholic schools grow up in an environment replete with religious imagery to remind them of their creator, their redeemer, his mother and so much more. Work by artists from across the continents and centuries is carefully selected to enrich and inspire. From ancient icons to modern sculpture and paintings, children may find that the art in their schools will help to lift their minds and hearts to God. I remember so clearly the picture of God sitting on a cloud which adorned the back of the classroom door opposite my desk when I was seven. He had a long white beard and was surrounded by angels. Under the picture, in easy-to-read print, were the words of the Morning Offering, that prayer through which we offer to God all the 'prayers, works, suffering and joys of this day'. It made me feel that God was watching over us and keeping us safe as we studied. It is through simple images such as these that young minds may be gently alerted to the presence of God in the world, and as they grow older they may come to a more profound understanding of the complexity of artists' rich and varied portrayals of faith.

Children attending Catholic schools are also alerted to the literature of faith and as they mature they will be made aware of the huge body of thought and understanding about faith available to us. With the right influences they may come to enjoy reading and exploring the thoughts of those who have come before them. At a time when I was trying to understand what life was all about I remember reading a book called *Costing Not Less Than Everything*.[3] It was an easy read which took me through author John Dalrymple's experience of being a man of faith. It made me think, and that is what children need to do if they are to grow in faith.

Catholic schools also provide the opportunity to participate in carefully created liturgy: and children will grow up learning to sing hymns and to make music in honour of God, who so loves them. They will learn about their faith and about Jesus' life and work. They will come to know his words – words that will stay with them and provide comfort during difficult times in their lives. They will have the opportunity to know personally priests, sisters and chaplains – those whose lives are specially dedicated to the work of God – as people to whom they can talk about all the things which exercise their young minds as they work out what they want to do with their lives. They will be exposed to the great history of the Church and will come to know that they are part of a global Church of 1.2 million people; that almost everywhere in the world they will meet and be able to pray and work with fellow Catholics. The Catholic Church has a proud tradition of social justice, and throughout their schooldays children will play a part in that work: fundraising for the poor and hungry, helping those less privileged than they are and learning to see

---

3 John Dalrymple, *Costing Not Less Than Everything: Notes on Holiness Today* (London: Darton, Longman & Todd Ltd, 1975).

all the children of the world as their brothers and sisters. In secondary school they will have the opportunity to engage in the Church's benevolent work across the world more directly, by building houses, schools and working in orphanages; experiences through which they may become better people and come to understand that they can make a difference in the world.

Over the past few years an energetic lobby for secular education has led to surveys in Ireland seeking to establish the extent to which parents, initially in five areas, want to have a greater choice in patronage of their schools. A survey of parents in 306 Catholic schools in Ireland returned a recommendation for change in the patronage arrangements in just twenty-eight of those schools – 9 per cent. Another survey with a response rate of about 20 per cent over twenty-three areas expressed an opinion in favour of change that amounted to between 2.2 per cent and 8 per cent of parents with children in schools in the areas taken into account. The reality is that there is not overwhelming support for non-denominational schools in Ireland. In Northern Ireland the situation is similar: there, approximately 7 per cent of children are educated in the integrated sector despite the commendable work which has been done to support the creation of further integrated schools and the government's continued support of such enterprise.

Conclusion

Very often, non-Catholics will opt to send their children to Catholic schools because of their academic, cultural, social and sporting records of achievement. Millions of parents across the world have faith in Catholic schools, trusting in them as places where their children will be cared for, nurtured in faith, experience sacrament and liturgy, grow aware of their responsibilities and role in matters of social justice and fairness and see daily examples of people – from the members of the board, to teachers, cleaners, caretakers and dinner ladies – who love God and try to walk in his way. They are confirmed in the understanding, above all, that they and their children are loved by God and made for eternal love. That is why we should recognise the value of our Catholic schools, send our children to them and do all we can to preserve them to ensure that our children's children too will have access to such invaluable and formative lived experience of faith.

What the Catholic School Has to Offer

Amalee Meehan

Even Marge Simpson believes that Catholic schools have something special to offer. When Bart is blamed for a silly prank and expelled from Springfield Elementary School, she enrols him in St Jerome's Catholic School, but as Bart and Homer find out, Catholic school has much more to offer than good discipline. Through Fr Sean (voiced by Liam Neeson) they encounter understanding, hospitality, fun and good learning – just some of the hallmarks of a Catholic education.

In Ireland, parents choose Catholic school for a variety of reasons. A 2008 study showed that parents who send their child to Catholic schools[1] actively choose a school with a religious denomination.[2] However, a more recent study (2011) found that the factors that most influenced parents include an education that encourages their imagination, the discipline in the school, geographical proximity and the quality of the education provided by that school.[3] The quality

---

1   In both the 2008 and 2011 reports, the phrase 'Catholic schools' denotes primary schools under the patronage of a Catholic bishop.

2   Irish Catholic Bishops' Conference, *Parental Understandings of Patronage* (2011), http://www.catholicschools.ie/2011/09/28/parental-understandings-of-patronage/ [accessed 10 May 2013].

3   The 2011 study was conducted with principals, teachers, priests, assessors, pastoral council members and pupils, who participated in a series of focus group discussions in February and March 2011. It was one element of a wider consultative process carried out as part of the Church's internal reflection on Catholic primary school patronage. In his Executive Summary, *Parental Understandings of Patronage* (2011), researcher Eoin O'Mahony outlines how the rationale for the study arises from work conducted with a much larger set of parents in 2007/08 around factors determining school choice.

issue includes provision of a schooling experience that parents wish their child to have.

The 2011 study also reveals consensus on many different themes, including a conviction that the Catholic school has unique, identifiable characteristics and is considered valid and valued in modern Ireland.[4] Of course, the defining feature of any Catholic school, indeed any faith school, is belief in God.

In this essay I attempt to explore the Catholic belief in God, how it informs the spirit of a Catholic school and affects the type of education found there. To do this, I draw from Catholic Christian theology and from my own experience working with voluntary second-level schools. I go on to outline the significant threat to this type of education, especially at second level. My hope is to give those making choices about schools and children an appreciation of what the Catholic school can offer. A secondary hope is to raise awareness that if reasonable action to preserve the sector is not taken quickly, the choice to send one's child to a Catholic second-level school will not be there for some, perhaps for many, in the near future.

The Question of God Will Not Go Away

Every education philosophy reflects beliefs about meaning and purpose. There is no such thing as a value-neutral education. All schools express an ethos by their choices, actions and attitudes. Whether established by the state or by some voluntary group, all schools espouse a particular vision of the human person and of life in the world. What is of ultimate value to the short human life is of universal concern.

Faith schools deal with questions of meaning, purpose and ultimate value with reference to God (although language for the

---

4 Irish Catholic Bishops' Conference, *Report on Catholic Primary Schools* (2011) http://www.catholicschools.ie/2011/10/07/executive-summary-report-on-catholic-primary-schools/ [accessed 11 May 2013].

mystery Christians term 'God' differs among faith traditions). Regardless of whether an individual believer is convinced, questioning or unconvinced, for believers in general the question of God is important. This becomes a major contributing factor to a school ethos or, to use the language of the Education Act 1998, a school 'characteristic spirit'.[5]

School Characteristic Spirit

Every school has a characteristic spirit, either by design or by default. There is no such thing as teaching and learning from a neutral standpoint. Faith-based schools, like all schools, have a legal responsibility and right to uphold a school ethos or characteristic spirit. In Catholic schools, this characteristic spirit is rooted in Catholic Christianity, which gives rise to certain principles or ways of looking at the world. It contributes in many specific ways to the type of education offered there.

Characteristic spirit can be like an iceberg – only the tip obvious, the invisible bulk providing the anchor. Because of its theological tradition, the Catholic school can name its anchors. The invisible bulk is easily made visible to anyone – supporter and critic alike – who looks below the surface. When debating the question of what type of school to choose for their children, parents can therefore consider the ways a Catholic spirit vivifies a school and its lived-out, everyday dimensions.

Later I will outline two of the fundamental anchors of Catholic Christianity and how they give rise to the characteristic spirit in Catholic schools. However, in order to understand Catholic schools, we must first try to understand what the Catholic Christian tradition means by the word 'God'.

---

5   Department of Education, Education Act (1998), http://www.irishstatutebook. ie/1998/en/act/pub/0051/sec0015.html#sec15 [accessed 2 June 2013].

God as Mystery

To begin, 'God' does not refer to a person. There is not some person out there, older, wiser and more powerful than the average person whose name is 'God'. Theologian Michael Himes explains the use of the term 'God' as shorthand, which functions in Christian theology almost as x functions in algebra. When working through an algebraic problem, one's focus is x, but x is shorthand for the thing one doesn't know. In a similar way, God is the name of the mystery that lies at the root of all that exists. Because we are talking about ultimate mystery we must not forget that we will never have the last word on God; never have anything close to complete comprehension. But that must not stop us trying.[6]

God as Love

Like any great religious tradition, Christianity maintains that while it cannot say everything about the mystery that is God, it can say something. As there is no absolutely right way to talk about God, Himes uses the phrase 'least wrong way'. For Christians, the least wrong way to imagine God is God as love.[7] The New Testament repeats this over and over again in the parables and ministry of Jesus, but it is said most forthrightly in one of its very late documents, the first letter of John. In chapter 4 of this letter we read that God is *agape* – self-giving love (1 Jn 4:8, 16).

The Greek word chosen to describe the love that is God is curious. The word *agape* denotes a particular kind of love. *Agape* is a purely other-directed love, one that seeks nothing in return. It is translated well as 'self-gift' – the gift of oneself to another without expectation, regardless of whether the gift is accepted or rejected. The cornerstone of Catholic schools then – the primary reason they even exist – is

---

6   Michael J. Himes and D. P. McNeill, *Doing the Truth in Love: Conversations about God, Relationships, and Service* (New York: Paulist Press 1995).

7   Ibid.

to bring people into contact with the God that is self-giving love. This becomes increasingly important as education is more and more commodified.[8] An instrumentalised education driven by economic imperatives may satisfy the market but it will never suffice for holistic education, in and of the person. Authentic Catholic education is an antidote to instrumentalisation because at its heart is the person, in and of themselves. An education that humanises rather than instrumentalises is just as good, if not better, for society; it puts things in the right order. When we are really loved in and of ourselves, it frees us to genuinely love in return.

How this Love is Expressed

We see glimmers of agapic love in the world around us. It is sometimes beautifully depicted in the world of children's popular culture. For instance, in *The Lion King*, Mufasa gives his life to save his only son – little lion cub Simba. The wonderful children's book *Guess How Much I Love You* has Big Nutbrown Hare showing Little Nutbrown Hare a love that has no bounds. We can also see agapic love at work in our schools. Since 2008, I have worked with CEIST (Catholic Education, an Irish Schools Trust), first as faith development coordinator and latterly as faith leadership and governance coordinator.[9] Of the many

---

8   Kathleen Lynch, Bernie Grummell and Dympna Devine, *New Managerialism in Education: Commercialization, Carelessness and Gender* (London: Palgrave Macmillan, 2012).

9   In 2007, five Catholic religious congregations that have been engaged in post-primary education for over three and a half centuries – Daughters of Charity, Presentation Sisters, Sisters of the Christian Retreat, Sisters of Mercy and Missionaries of the Sacred Heart – in the spirit of their founders, together established CEIST. CEIST provides a new moral and legal trustee framework enabling their schools to continue to offer post-primary Catholic education into the future as a viable option and as an integral part of the Irish school system. CEIST is built on the founding vision of the five congregations, emphasising the dignity and rights of the human person, empowering the most vulnerable in society and enabling young people to become catalysts for social transformation throughout the world. For more details see www.ceist.ie.

practical examples of CEIST schools I have witnessed, I present just two that mirror *agape* love.

School A

School A is a girls' school located in a small, very deprived parish, which is host to feuding drug families in a socially divided city. About 20 per cent of the students in School A come from this socio-economic background.

When the feuding started some years ago, the number of children enrolling in the local feeder primary school declined rapidly. Numbers in School A dropped accordingly. However, many of the teachers' daughters continued and still continue to attend this school. Their success and the success of so many of the girls who attend School A is a positive beacon in a place where it is both needed and deserved. This message of faith in the school reverberates throughout the wider community.

During this period, School A not only maintained its numbers, it also developed a very strong reputation, locally and nationally, in debating, shows, musicals and choir. This is largely due to the enormous generosity and commitment of both the principal and staff and their shared belief that the school should and can be a vibrant community of hope, especially in the socio-economic context in which it operates.

The school has also developed close links with the local parish, and through the parish, the local community. Liturgy, understood and celebrated as an important unifying symbolic activity, is very important in the school. To my mind, however, the annual trip to Lourdes is particularly significant. This trip, an annual highlight in the school calendar, is open to every senior student. Some years ago, the chaplain – a Mercy Sister who gives her time and commitment on a voluntary basis – managed to secure a major sponsor in making an annual donation. The local congregation of the Sisters of Mercy also makes a contribution. The chaplain and staff organise fundraising activities, such as bag packing, so that the students also raise money. Through the heartfelt generosity and commitment of the school community, every student who wants to, can travel and everyone who travels can contribute towards the cost.

School B

School B is a large school serving a small town and its extensive rural hinterland. It is not the only school in town. Some years ago, the HSE approached School B and requested that it accept a student who had a troubled history. Patrick (not his real name), aged 15, had been through a number of foster homes. He talked to no one. In fact, he shut off all possible communication by means of headphones constantly in his ears. Patrick was 'alone in the yard and the assembly area'.[10] Both his attendance and punctuality were erratic.

Despite severe cutbacks in successive budgets, School B has heroically maintained its standards in the pastoral care of students, especially those most in need. Since the DES abolished the position of Home School Liaison some years ago, the post has been filled on a part-time voluntary basis by a Presentation Sister. Although guidance counsellors are no longer ex quota and most schools are struggling to provide any sort of guidance counselling, School B has prioritised this service through fundraising and the goodwill of those on staff who are qualified in this area. Along with senior management and year heads, these people form a care team which serves the students in ways one can never fully know.

In short, School B has a highly evolved practice of vigilance, care and early intervention which has transformed the lives of countless students, including Patrick. In his particular case, a small but committed group – including staff, his (new) foster mother,

---

10 The year head in conversation with the author.

and a social worker who was involved with the local hurling team – galvanised around the year head. They set to work to support him day after difficult day.

During a recent visit to School B I witnessed Patrick, open and happy, chat easily with the principal and banter with his peers. The year head described how Patrick 'has light in his eyes, communicates well with people and has self-belief. He asks for help and will identify difficulties in his path. He hasn't missed a day in months and has ended up loving school. He has gone on [with a quiz team] to win an All Ireland medal … is well regarded by his class and has good friends. He is aiming to pursue a course in UCD. We will always admire him for how he has overcome so many obstacles in his life at this tender age.'[11]

Of course such experiences are not exclusive to CEIST schools. What is noteworthy, however, is that in both of these cases the inspiration behind what they are doing and why they are doing it is directly linked to the Catholic ethos.[12] The studies of sociologist Robert Bellah et al. conclude that acting compassionately and reaching out to those in need is not sustainable without recourse to the impetus or source of the virtue. When we lose the ability to connect our good behaviours and concerns for the common good to the source, those very behaviours and concerns begin to diminish.[13] It is very clear in the minds of the principals of schools A and B that their attitudes, choices and actions are inspired by their faith – the same faith which informs the school characteristic spirit.

From a Catholic worldview perspective, the encounter with compassion and commitment as described above is an encounter

---

11   Ibid.

12   The principal and chaplain of School A in conversation with the author; the principal and some staff members of School B in conversation with the author.

13   Robert N. Bellah, Richard Madsen, William M. Sullivan, Ann Swindler and Steven M. Tipton, *Habits of the Heart: Individualism and Commitment in American Life* (New York: Harper & Row, 1985).

with *agape*. Where there is love, there is God. Where there is God there is love. Deeply ingrained in the fabric of many Catholic schools, it is something sensed and encountered, rather than written up in brochures or advertised on websites. Yet it can make a real difference to the education of a child. I noted earlier that the characteristic spirit of a school deeply affects the type of education it offers. Here I consider two anchors of Catholic Christianity and the visible ways they can vivify the characteristic spirit of a school.

Meaning and Ultimate Meaning

The first anchor relates to the basic human question: does my life have meaning and if so where does it come from – do I give meaning to my own life or does my life have a meaning outside the one I give it? Meaning refers to the significance or import of something – why something matters. People make meaning in their lives in all sorts of ways, for instance through the experience of love and friendship, or by making a contribution to society. For the Christian, life has meaning and is meaningful. There is more to life than what we see on the surface. Part of the function of the Catholic school is to help students search for and discover this meaning for themselves.

A natural corollary to the question of meaning now adds the word 'ultimate'. Is there an ultimate meaning to my life and is there an ultimate purpose to existence? How one answers these age-old questions will be predicated on one's belief or lack thereof in God. If one does not believe in God, there is no ultimate significance to one's sense of meaning, value or purpose – this life is all there is. Belief in God, on the other hand, presumes there is an ultimate dimension to life. Life has significance beyond what we ourselves notice or attach. Rather than being invented, meaning, value and purpose are discovered through faith in God. How one views that God then becomes an essential question. If one believes in God, then one's image of God is very important.

The Christian belief in God

For Catholic Christians, the Mystery of God that is self-giving love is revealed in Jesus Christ. Jesus is the face of God. Through knowing him we come to know God. This has huge importance in a world where disconnected images of God can sometimes emerge. One such image is that of the Cosmic Computer Player. This is a god who sits on high, makes judgments on his subjects and punishes at will. Like a player sitting at an enormous cosmic computer, this God randomly pushes buttons that can have catastrophic consequences, from the death of a child to tsunami wave destruction. A second anti-Christian image is that of the Therapeutic God, whose sole function is to make us feel good about ourselves. This God feeds our hunger for affirmation without ever challenging destructive behaviours or helping us to discern how best to grow into the people we were made to become.

The Christian image of God

The Christian God came among us as a baby, born in the humblest of circumstances, raised by a loving family and a mother who encouraged and stayed with him until the moment he died. This God taught of a reign of love and peace and justice for all people and all of creation. This God suffered and died at the hands of a mob and then overcame death through resurrection. This God lives on in us – we are his hands and feet, his mind, heart and strength – the Body of Christ in the world today.

A Catholic school would therefore be failing this cornerstone belief if it did not introduce children to God through the New Testament, especially the Jesus stories of the gospels; if it did not teach children Christian prayers, especially the prayers to Jesus and his Blessed Mother; if it did not remember the Jesus stories in appropriate ways by following the liturgical year and if it did not embody the values of this God who is love (1 Jn 4:8).

Let's unpack, for instance, the symbolic importance of the crib at Christmas. The Christmas crib is the visible image of the birth of the Christ child. It can teach the profound implications of the incarnation to a five year old just as it can strike a chord of remembrance with an indifferent adult. The crib teaches that Christmas is not simply about trees and decorations, new clothes and presents, quietly questioning the contemporary acceptance of acquisition as a goal. It speaks of those humble beginnings and encourages us to look beyond the manipulation of media advertising to the values that Christmas stands for – values that are surely acceptable to those of any religious tradition and none; that regardless of circumstance, we can always help those in need, that the love of family is irreplaceable, that true kings can emerge even from the most humble of beginnings, that the stranger has much to teach and the lowly have much to tell. If we really want to teach people about inclusion, what better place to start?

In a Catholic school the nativity story cannot be presented as one Christmas story among many. It is *the* Christmas story. It is the story of the incarnation – a central mystery for Christians. The baby in the manger is often depicted with his arms wide open in welcome; only from this central and rooted position can we be sure of our responsibility to do the same. This is the real nature of inclusion. Recent research identified the inclusive nature of Catholic schools as they continue to meet the needs of the marginalised in our society.[14] Here is the inspiration (considered so important by Bellah) for welcoming the privileged and the marginalised, the majestic and the ordinary, the familiar and the foreigner from a distant land, from a different religious tradition. When placed in this context, the evidence that interfaith and intercultural initiatives work best in schools where the

---

14 Irish Catholic Bishops' Conference, *Report on Catholic Primary Schools* (2011), http://www.catholicschools.ie/2011/10/07/executive-summary-report-on-catholic-primary-schools/ [accessed 11 May 2013].

Catholic population is most committed to its own religious practice makes perfect sense.[15]

Relationship with Jesus Christ

The belief in God as revealed to us in Jesus Christ is the inspiration, mission and vision of the Catholic school. Furthermore, Christians believe not only in Jesus Christ as the inspiration, but that relationship with him has the power to transform the human condition. We are all imperfect, incomplete. Every one of us is flawed and vulnerable. We are at our best and become our best in positive relationships, especially in positive relationship with God.

Therefore, loving relationship is the most important aspect to any Christian community, including the Catholic school. God is present in these sorts of relationships, for God is *agape*. And so the school places at its centre the invitation to personal relationship with Jesus Christ, the face of God. Children can learn to make sense of early, crucial, relational experiences such as friendship, betrayal, belonging or bullying in relation to Jesus the Son, the friend, the teacher, the refugee, the lost boy in the big city. Here is the God to whom children can relate, who wants to walk the journey with each one of us, who calls us to grow into the persons we were made to be and gives us the strength and wherewithal to do exactly that.

If our education system is to avoid instrumentalisation and instead foster the whole child, it needs to allow for questions of meaning and ultimate meaning. Children need access to resources to live and explore these dimensions of what it means to be human.

---

15 See for example John Coolahan, Caroline Hussey and Fionnuala Kilfeather, *The Forum on Patronage and Pluralism in the Primary Sector: Report of the Forum's Advisory Group*, http://www.education.ie/en/Press-Events/Conferences/ Patronage-and-Pluralism-in-the-Primary-Sector/The-Forum-on-Patronage-and-Pluralism-in-the-Primary-Sector-Report-of-the-Forums-Advisory-Group.pdf [accessed 4 June 2013].

An emerging difference in school identity is concerned with this question of ultimacy. Given their theistic foundation, Catholic schools will naturally allow for this dimension of human life. An instrumentalised education that ignores mysteries, meaning and the possibility of ultimacy, deprives adolescent spirituality of otherness beyond their comprehension, and confines their world to the instant and immediate. In a society where teenage suicide is very much a reality, can we afford to ignore the psycho-social effects of this type of education?[16]

Sacramental Imagination

A second Christian pillar that can contribute enormously to the characteristic spirit of a Catholic school is that of sacramental imagination. Let me introduce this concept through the work of C. S. Lewis. When Lewis was asked why he had written *The Chronicles of Narnia*, he replied that he wanted children to experience something of 'the deeper magic of life'.[17] By way of his stories, he hoped that children would experience God and encounter the power and mystery of Christ through the character of Aslan. The Narnia stories were written in a way that would engage with the real lives of children – their curiosity and wonder and sense of unfairness, their experiences of friendship and betrayal. Moreover, these stories were to awaken children's sense of the sacred. In short, C. S. Lewis wanted to share the central Christian belief that the presence of God can be discerned in all dimensions of life – the sacramental imagination.

16 See for examples Des O'Neill, 'We Need to Talk About Spirituality in Healthcare', *Irish Times* (19 June 2012), http://www.irishtimes.com/news/health/we-need-to-talk-about-spirituality-in-healthcare-1.1067314 and Patricia Casey, 'The Psycho-Social Benefits of Religious Practice' (2009), http://www.ionainstitute.ie/assets/files/Religious_practice-1.pdf [accessed 10 May 2013].
17 Geoffrey Marshall-Taylor, 'The Narnia Effect, the Deeper Magic', *The Way Supplement* 86 (1996): pp. 63–9.

A truly Catholic education encourages the habit of seeing beneath or behind what is obvious and noticing the sacred. Sometimes the scales can fall from our eyes all of a sudden. For instance, the birth of a child might prompt a profound experience of a life force, and for a moment we feel an extraordinary connection to God. However, rather than a momentary or 'out of the blue' effect, Catholic Christianity attempts to notice the presence of God in ordinary and everyday life. God's presence is not confined to a major event, to churches and holy places, or indeed to formal religious education; we can experience God through the bits and pieces of our daily lives.

A false understanding

The belief that God is present in the ordinary bits and pieces of everyday life has often been lost in time and translation. The insight of theologian Richard Gaillardetz helps to make this point. In the illustration below (fig. 1), the emphasis is on the distance and difference between God and the rest of the world.[18] The central point is that God is an individual, out there beyond our planet.

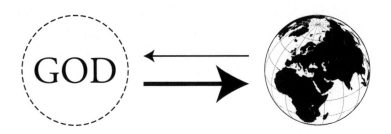

Fig. 1[19]

---

18 Richard Gaillardetz, *Transforming Our Days: Spirituality, Community, and Liturgy in a Technological Culture* (New York: The Crossroad Publishing Company, 2000).

19 Ibid., p. 48.

Gaillardetz believes that this is the way many Christians think about God today. In this framework, God is outside the world and responds from time to time to our prayers and intercessions. Our encounters with God only happen at particular times, perhaps in response to prayer or when we attend Mass. In this way, life is organised in a dualistic manner between what is sacred and what is secular. So for instance, saying a prayer is sacred, while studying specific subjects, engaging in extracurricular activities or participating in sports are secular pursuits. Of course this is, at best, an impoverished notion of Christian theology and the characteristic spirit of the Catholic school.

A more authentic understanding

The second, and more authentically Christian perspective offered by Gaillardetz is radically different. In the second illustration, God is the 'loving and creative ground of our existence, the very atmosphere in whom we "live and move and have our being"' (Acts 17:28). In this image, the world is *in* God (fig. 2). Within this framework, there is no such thing as a dualistic notion of what is sacred or secular. *Everything* is sacred. Everything is in God and can disclose God's presence.

Fig. 2

From this theological perspective, everything in the life of a school – making friends, reading a poem, winning one day and losing the next – can disclose the presence and action of God. When the spirit is attuned, we can notice God any time, any place – in the corridor, classroom or chapel. Those moments when we notice or experience God in our lives are referred to as sacramental moments. A sacrament reveals the presence of God; it is a moment of encounter with Christ. While we might be familiar with the seven sacraments of the Catholic Church, we need to remember that everything can disclose God's presence and so everything can be sacramental.[20]

This sacramental imagination, or to use Lewis's phrase, the ability to see 'the deeper magic of life', is a natural capacity. However, it needs to be nurtured so that it becomes part of our way of being. Habits such as the ability to pause, to pray, to be present to oneself and to become aware of the presence of others and of God in our lives, foster the sacramental imagination. But they need practice. Just as a hurler completes thousands of drills so that a particular move becomes a natural part of his game, so the practice of habits forms a sacramental imagination. These habits, then, are fundamental to the daily rhythm of a Catholic school.

One real value of a sacramental imagination is the understanding of the whole world and all people as sacred. Everything and every person is capable of revealing God, and is worthy of justice and respect. This goes to the heart of what it means to be Catholic; the emphasis on social justice and service to others is part of the lived heritage of Catholic schools. In a 2012 ESRI survey, Catholic schools were deemed the most inclusive school type at primary level and more likely to enrol children from non-Irish backgrounds, from the Traveller community and with special needs.[21] The inclusivity of

---

20 See Michael J. Himes, *The Mystery of Faith: An Introduction to Catholicism* (Cincinnati, Ohio: St Anthony Messenger Press, 2004).

21 Merike Darmody, Emer Smyth and Selina McCoy, 'School Sector Variation Among Primary Schools in Ireland' (2012), http://www.esri.ie/__uuid/7c3b20b7-0671-43a1-8ca7-7d073b36e6d0/BKMNEXT221.pdf [accessed 3 June 2013].

the Catholic school as it continues to meet the needs of the local community and, in particular, the needs of the marginalised in our society, also emerged from research conducted by the Catholic Schools Partnership. It is therefore of little wonder that the Minister for Education and Skills noted that one of the strengths of the (predominantly Catholic) primary system has been that the local primary school has been very inclusive of all children within its community.[22]

However, it is clear that most Catholic voluntary secondary schools, including Schools A and B referred to earlier, are attempting to provide a quality education against the backdrop of slow starvation of the sector.

Financial Starvation

Voluntary secondary schools receive significantly lower funding from the DES than other secondary schools. According to Ferdia Kelly, General Secretary of the Association of Management of Catholic Secondary Schools (AMCSS), most people do not realise that schools in the Catholic secondary sector are severely disadvantaged in terms of annual grants compared with the other two post-primary sectors, Community and VEC.[23] For example, a Catholic school of four hundred pupils receives ninety euro per pupil less per annum than a similarly sized community school, and 212 euro per pupil less that than a four-hundred-pupil vocational school. On average over 30 per cent of annual expenditure in a Catholic voluntary school must be raised by the school itself through fundraising in the local community. In the current economic climate, such pressures on the school and local community are not sustainable. Ferdia Kelly contends that such

---

22 Coolahan et al. p. 84.

23 Ferdia Kelly, 'Catholic Voluntary Secondary Schools in Ireland: The Challenges for the Future', *Catholic Schools: Faith in Our Future*, Maedhbh Uí Chiagáin, ed. (Dublin: AMCSS, 2012).

fundraising pressure places a huge burden on school management, made up mainly of volunteers who give willingly of their time and expertise, and in turn reduces the time available for all of the other responsibilities that boards of management must undertake. In particular, there are serious concerns about the workload carried out by principals in Catholic secondary schools as a result of the absence of management and administrative supports exacerbated by recent cuts in funding.[24]

Curriculum Pressures

The severe cuts in finance and personnel in successive national budgets from 2009–12 has also resulted in curriculum pressures. Decreased finance and loss of staff means that many schools have been forced to reduce their curriculum. When the broadest choice of both subjects and programmes is no longer available in a school, parents and pupils have little choice but to look elsewhere. This flies in the face of recent research from the Catholic Schools Partnership which demonstrates the broad parental wish that their children are part of a community through the school, where the school is local to the home.[25]

Ferdia Kelly's remarks are a stark warning of the consequences:

> As a society in Ireland we need to address the reality that we are, in the name of austerity, creating a scenario where tracts of the Irish countryside will have no voluntary secondary school. Is this the type of society we want, where children are forced to spend long hours being transported out of their local school community where each pupil is known and cherished?[26]

---

24 Ibid., p. 13.
25 Irish Catholic Bishops' Conference, 'Parental Understandings of Patronage' (2011).
26 Ferdia Kelly, p. 12.

In short, the uneven playing field of funding has resulted in curriculum pressures, staff losses and budgetary deficits. However, the most obvious indicator of the forced hunger of the sector is the rate of school closures.

A Future of Love Lost

The decline in number of Catholic voluntary secondary schools has been rapid, with a decrease of over one hundred in the past twenty years. While many of these closures have resulted in community schools after amalgamation, the impact of this decline means that there are now areas of the country where there is no Catholic voluntary school available to parents. The school transport scheme provides support for those from minority religious traditions who desire a faith-based education, but to date no such facility is available to Catholic parents, with potentially devastating effects.

School C

Take for example the situation School C finds itself in. School C is about twenty miles from a city and has traditionally catered for a large rural area, with great success. The school has deep links with the community and is loved and respected by past pupils and their families, as evidenced by the number of people willing to serve on the board of management and give voluntarily of their time and resources. However, two new VEC schools are under construction on the outskirts of the city, between the city and School C. As a result, for the first year in living memory, enrolment for 2013 has noticeably dropped. This is directly related to the inequitable transport scheme. In other words, parents who wish to send their children to School C using the scheme but who live closer to the new VEC school will be offered transport only to the VEC school. One wonders how this sits with the Irish Constitution, which clearly supports parents in their choice of school.[27] Ironically, although state rhetoric is strongly in favour of plurality of provision, at second level we are witnessing an invidious erosion of choice.

A History of Love Lost

Contemporary political manoeuvering from the outside is not the only threat to Catholic schools. Indeed, sometimes an even greater threat comes from within. We cannot tell the full story of Catholic education in this country at present without reference to the failures of the past. A limited understanding of God and uncritical acceptance of the way the Church was evolving led to an anthropology and a way of looking at the world that was often more anti-Christian than Christian. Many people remember an education that cultivated mortification and punitive discipline, where learning and instilling fear went hand in hand. Ned Prendergast remarks, 'Whatever these failures were, they were ultimately failures in love.'[28]

However, as Prendergast warns, we have to be discerning about what blame we allow to be dumped on the Catholic school. He remembers a country that 'did not waste anesthetic in child dentistry' and describes mid-twentieth-century Ireland as 'a tough time, a tough society, [where] schools could be tough places'.[29] Memoirs

---

27 '42: The State acknowledges that the primary and natural educator of the child is the Family and guarantees to respect the inalienable right and duty of parents to provide, according to their means, for the religious and moral, intellectual, physical and social education of their children.' '42.2: Parents shall be free to provide this education in their homes or in private schools or in schools recognised or established by the State.' 'The State shall not oblige parents in violation of their conscience and lawful preference to send their children to schools established by the State, or to any particular type of school designated by the State.'

28 Ned Prendergast, 'What is Loved Survives', *Catholic Schools: Faith in Our Future*, p. 24.

29 Ibid., pp. 23–4.

such as *Angela's Ashes*[30] or *The Boy at the Gate*[31] are vivid reminders of just how tough it was. With institutional Church history and current state policy at our heels, never before have we been so challenged to articulate what a Catholic school stands for and what it can offer to the parents of Ireland today.

Conclusion

The Report on Catholic Primary Schools (2011) referred to in the opening paragraphs of this article identified a strong parental commitment to the continuation of Catholic primary schools.[32] However, while the public debate in this country focuses on primary schools, without a marked change in government policy, the Catholic second-level sector is in danger of dying on its feet. If we want a Catholic second-level option in the future, we need to redress the imbalance. This is both urgent and important in the face of an increasingly instrumentalised view of education. What was gained over centuries will otherwise be lost in a generation, and the loss will have consequences both foretold and as yet unseen.

The cornerstone of Catholic schools – the primary reason they even exist – is to bring people into contact with the God that is self-giving love. The two anchors I put forward suggest that a Catholic school is one which connects people with God, revealed in Jesus Christ. This God is very close, in and of the world, if only we had eyes to see. A truly Catholic school can open our eyes to the presence of God in the ordinary and everyday hopes and successes, sorrows and disappointments of life. As Prendergast outlines:

> Although God is always knocking on the door of the human heart, we must play our part in introducing young people to

---

30 Frank McCourt, *Angela's Ashes* (New York: Scribner, 1996).

31 Danny Ellis, *The Boy at the Gate* (London: Transworld Ireland, 2012).

32 Irish Catholic Bishops' Conference, *Report on Catholic Primary Schools* (2011).

the one who gives a Christian school its name, its heart, its prophetic imagination, and its Catholic invitation that all are welcome.[33]

God is always seeking out the human heart. Catholic schools help those hearts attune to the one who searches for them. For many people, Catholic school has been a place of grace. This is true of the past as well as the present. I conclude with the words of John McGahern, a writer never slow to critique the institutions or establishment of his day. Reflecting on his time in Presentation College, Carrick-on-Shannon, McGahern writes:

I look back on those years as the beginning of an adventure that has never stopped. Each day as I cycled towards Carrick was an anticipation of delights. The fear and drudgery of school disappeared. Without realising it, through the pleasures of the mind, I was beginning to know and to love the world. The Brothers took me in, sat me down, and gave me tools. I look back on my time there with nothing but gratitude, as years of luck and privilege – and of grace, actual grace.[34]

---

33 Prendergast, p. 27.
34 McGahern, John, *Memoir* (London: Faber and Faber, 2005), p. 171.

The Personal and Communal Nature of Faith: A Parent's Experience of Catholic Education

Orla Walsh

Some years ago, my family was celebrating a birthday in a local restaurant. Having been shown to our table we were presented with five menus, two of which were kids' menus for the younger children. Displaying a modicum of righteous indignation, our middle son requested an *à la carte* menu and stated that as he had celebrated his Confirmation and was now an 'adult in the eyes of the Church', he felt entitled to dine as one. Funny as it was, this incident demonstrated that the Confirmation ceremony had really meant something to him: that he was now shaking off his childish coil and wished to 'blossom into a future' and embrace his new role as a full and active member of the Catholic Church. We had already chosen a Catholic school for our eldest son, so it was quite natural that this young lad would follow.

A Catholic School

There are many definitions of what the essence of a Catholic school truly is. Most recently *Share the Good News: The National Directory for Catechesis* tells us that the Catholic school 'promotes tolerance, respect and inclusiveness. Its educational perspective is Catholic and ecumenical by nature and open to inter-religious and inter-cultural dialogues.' It goes on to note that a Catholic school promotes the holistic formation of young people in 'the construction of a world based on dialogue and search for community ... on the mutual acceptance of differences rather than on their opposition.'[1]

This was my own experience of attending a Catholic school, and now, over thirty years later, I can quite honestly say that it has also been my children's experience. The Catholic school extends a daily invitation to reach one's full potential in an environment that respects dignity and celebrates possibilities. Recently there has been what I can only call a disconnect between the language used to describe the experience of a denominational school and the reality that is a denominational school. Words such as 'indoctrination' and 'proselytism' have emerged in the conversation. Yet to find a single denominational school in Ireland that indoctrinates or proselytises its students is most unlikely. Moreover, the teaching staff and management of Irish schools spend their time ensuring that their students are educated and cared for in a deeply respectful environment, encouraging each student to become fully human and fully alive for themselves in their relationships with each other and in their relationship with God. This 'faith framing' is the added value that a denominational school provides.

---

1   Irish Episcopal Conference, *Share the Good News: National Directory for Catechesis in Ireland* (Dublin: Veritas, 2010), p. 143.

Primary School

Traditionally, Irish primary schools are supported by different Christian denominations, and local children attend the local school established by the community. Like many families, we greatly value and respect the Irish language and heritage; thus choosing a *gaelscoil* with a Catholic ethos for the first eight years of our children's education felt a very natural choice.

It is important to add that the sacramental preparation of our children in Gaelscoil na Bóinne has been indicative of the time, effort and energy so many Catholic primary schools put into their pupils' preparation for and celebration of the sacraments. It is also worth adding that for First Holy Communion, this particular school advocates a policy whereby each child wears a white robe over their choice of clothes for the day. To my mind, this is a most dignified symbol of what is actually taking place during the celebration of the sacrament of First Eucharist.

In the recent publication *Toward Mutual Ground: Pluralism, Religious Education and Diversity in Irish Schools,* Gareth Byrne reminds us that

> school, along with home and parish or other community, plays a significant part as the natural environment within which primary-level children find support, not only for their everyday physical, emotional and social requirements but also for their everyday religious, moral and spiritual needs.

This year our daughter was especially taken with her teacher's Easter preparation and we noted that the exploration and engagement with material around the Easter story had caused her to, in her own words, 'think about Jesus in a different way'. This supportive voice from outside the home greatly heartened us and was one that was clearly heard by our daughter, who wished to participate in all the

Easter ceremonies and freely entered into discussion about them. For us this is a powerful testimony to the faith development she receives at school and the support we receive in turn. This moment echoes Byrne when he writes that 'children at primary level learn through the local and the particular'.[2]

Denominational School

When it comes to religion and beliefs, there is a huge variation in language available to describe our schools. There are multi-denominational, inter-denominational, non-denominational and denominational schools. This language, often in need of clarification, owes its origin to our Irish Christian heritage. The Department of Education and Science states that the 'aim of education is to contribute towards the development of all aspects of the individual, including aesthetic, creative, critical, cultural, emotional, intellectual, moral, physical, political, social and spiritual development'. Like many other schools, the Catholic school fulfils this mandate and roots all the various strands of development within the framework of a Christocentric faith. Catholic schools encourage the personal and communal nature of faith. Thus faith is made explicit in the daily life of the school. The daily routine works within our core values as parents and supports their articulation in faith. It is this choice that we as parents have made for our children as it is our opinion that having a framework of faith serves to enhance a student's appreciation of the overall aim of education and increases his or her ability to engage with the different strands. Exploring the rich heritage of the Irish Christian tradition is to the fore in the religious education syllabus, thus 'responsible citizenship is well served by educated people of faith

---

2   Gareth Byrne, 'Encountering and Engaging With Religon and Belief: The Contemporary Contribution of Religious Education in Schools', *Toward Mutual Ground: Pluralism, Religious Education and Diversity in Irish Schools*, Gareth Byrne and Patricia Kiernan, eds (Dublin: Columba Press, 2013), p. 212.

holding their own beliefs and convictions in a way that contributes to the common good'.

Good for You

Speaking at the announcement of funding for the new Jigsaw programme created by Headstrong – an evidence-based, integrated model designed to strengthen a community's capacity to support young people's mental health – Kathleen Lynch TD, Minister of State at the Department of Health, said that the government wished to be proactive in developing and promoting better services to support the mental health of young people. The Minister went on to acknowledge that young people up to the age of twenty-four are in a critical period of development, hence it is crucial to identify any issues at an early stage as research states 'that early and brief intervention prevents people from experiencing lifetimes of pain and lost opportunities'.

While certainly not wishing to reduce faith to a 'healthier option', I can speak on behalf of myself and a large extended family who enthuse about the benefits of spirituality and prayer in one's life. I used to think that as long as my children were happy I would be too. However life has taught me different. Happiness and sadness ebb and flow like the tide, so now when I am asked what I want for my children, I say 'peace'. It is peace of mind I wish for them and peace at their core. It is only when I am at peace that I can be truly mindful of the presence of God in my life, and so too with them. I wish that they attain a deep peace to sustain their essence and authenticity as they be still and know God. Yeats's beautiful words ring true: 'for peace comes dropping slow'.[3] The value of learning how to reflect and 'be' in the quiet moments is indeed a skill that calls for continuous practice and a dedicated space in the stressful world of modernity.

---

3   W. B. Yeats, 'The Lake Isle of Innisfree'.

Offering the space for reflection and prayer is very much part of the day in a Catholic school and as such lends support to our family's decision to pray with our kids. As Brenda Lealman writes:

> A capacity for religious and spiritual awareness is innate in the human species, but this needs to be activated and may otherwise remain dormant or inert for long periods of time, perhaps even for a lifetime. For this capacity to be activated in any individual he or she needs to learn some mode of expression; otherwise that awareness may never reach the level of conscious reflection.[4]

It is wholly in keeping with our faith that our children are given time, space and indeed resources to activate and sustain their spirituality in their adolescent years – the most formative years of their lives.

Numerous case studies have also found that developing a spirituality through prayer has become a great source of strength and hope for those who have experienced great suffering, helping them to maintain their mental and physical health.[5] The call to peace and prayer has been the bedrock of Catholic spirituality. Indeed my alma mater, Loreto College, Cavan, is immersed in a strong Ignation spirituality and it was in school that I first learned to meditate and take some quiet time in the chapel each day. Acquiring this skill can lead to personal resilience, with the ability to create a space in one's day to be mindful of the presence of God at work. For me, Catholic schooling nurtures this possibility, and supports the expression of faith in day-to-day reality.

---

4   Brenda Lealman, 'Grottos, Ghettos and City of Glass: Conversations about Spirituality', *British Journal of Religious Education* 8.2 (1986): pp. 65–72.

5   For example, Ellen G. Levine, Caryn Aviv, Grace Yoo, Cheryl Ewing and Alfred Au, 'The Benefits of Prayer on Mood and Well-being of Breast Cancer Survivors', *Support Care Cancer* 17.3 (March 2009): pp 295–306; Jacinta Kelly, 'Spirituality as a Coping Mechanism', *Dimensions of Critical Care Nursing* 23.4 (July/August 2004): pp. 162–8.

Holistic

The Catholic Bishops *Vision '08* document advises us that 'Catholic schools seek to reflect a distinctive vision of life and a corresponding philosophy of education. This is based on the gospel of Jesus Christ.'[6] Because Catholic schools have a holistic philosophy of education, each student is called to become all that they can be in a caring and supportive environment. We know that many Catholic schools are famous for their GAA football and hurling, basketball, volleyball, rugby, athletics, musicals, debating, choirs, charity work and much more. As a school community they aspire to build an inviting, stimulating and mutually respectful environment where students are encouraged and empowered to develop their gifts and talents in an integrated and mutually respectful way. A returned missionary once told me that Catholic schools were instantly recognisable in developing countries. I inquired if this was because of the symbolic nature of the cross and he replied, 'No, not always, it was the pitches and running tracks that marked out our schools as different.' In a world where God is often missing, and not missed, Catholic schools work to espouse their core values and live their mission statements.

Religious Education

Religious education in a post-primary school is defined by a range of knowledge, understandings, skills and attitudes as set out by the state syllabus. It is curriculum focussed and optional as an exam subject for all students. Students are encouraged to recognise, respect, appreciate and engage with religious education. This may be realised through 'learning about' religions, which might also be described as a phenomological approach to teaching religious education: the learner acquires a rich religious literacy but does not experience the exploration of faith. A denominational approach also adds a 'learning

---

6   Irish Episcopal Conference, *Vision '08: A Vision for Catholic Education in Ireland* (Dublin: Veritas, 2008).

from' position, which can be seen as a more inclusive pedagogy of religious education. Suzanne Dillon from the Department of Education and Skills notes that 'a fundamental principle of inclusive practice is that all children should learn together. They learn from and with each other'.[7] In a faith context this is equally so, and in agreement with Gareth Byrne there is a value in 'learning within' one's faith community: 'the denominational school facilitates the religious education and formation of pupils *within* a particular Christian faith'.[8] This means, for example, that the liturgical year is celebrated in school, offering students the chance to have a participative role in prayer services and liturgies as well as affording them the space to have quiet time and reflect. Management and teaching staff promote tolerance and respect for people of all faiths and of no faith. Hence in a Catholic school religious education is not only a core subject but also a lived experience.

In a climate of growing secularism, Catholic schools promote pluralism in society where young people of other religions and beliefs are respected and supported in their own journey of faith. For Catholic students in a Catholic school their faith is rooted in the characteristic spirit of the school and the founding story shapes that culture. The progressive sisters and teachers in Loreto College were hugely inspirational in my adolescent years. The story of founder Mary Ward impacted on my own faith story. Through it I was made aware that we are each called to live out our unique gift embodied in 'freedom, justice, sincerity and joy'. In retrospect I can see that this did have an impression on my adolescence in the 1980s. Yet it is important to say that choosing a Catholic school for our own children is not limited

---

7   Suzanne Dillon, 'Religious Education at Second Level in Ireland', *Toward Mutual Ground: Pluralism, Religious Education and Diversity in Irish Schools*, p. 73.

8   Gareth Byrne, 'Encountering and Engaging With Religion and Belief: The Contemporary Contribution of Religious Education in Schools', *Toward Mutual Ground: Pluralism, Religious Education and Diversity in Irish Schools*, p. 213.

to nostalgia or a vague wish for them to 'have what I had', and that to promote discussion and a culture of responsibility around parental choice in choosing a Catholic school for a son or daughter is to be encouraged and indeed welcomed.

Who Are They?

I often look at my children and ask this question. We are so alike and bonded in many ways but we are intrinsically different in so many others. They are Celtic Tiger cubs and digital natives. They have a short concentration span and long hair, huge tolerance for difference and small appetite for injustice; they are much more socialised and confident that I ever was. That said, I didn't own a laptop that could crash, so my work was never lost; my phone was in a green kiosk and my friends were real and fewer (I had about twenty compared to my two sons' combined 854 Facebook 'friends').

So who are they, these offspring I have loved from the moment they were born? Two boys and a girl, two teenagers and a nine-year-old who thinks she is twenty. According to Piaget, the two adolescents have developed formal operational thought.[9] This is of real interest to me as it means they have developed the capacity to think abstractly about key concepts in our faith. In addition, they are at a point in their lives where the adults they will become are beginning to emerge, and so they may well be experiencing some level of what Erikson famously entitled an 'identity crisis'.[10] We know that adolescents are involved in a process of restructuring and reshaping their identity. Whether this leads to a crisis or not depends on each individual's genetic make-up, heritage and environment. It is important to note that research has identified that perhaps, in the

9   Jean Piaget, quoted in James W. Fowler, *Stages of Faith: The Psychology of Human Development and the Quest For Meaning* (New York: HarperOne, 1981), p. 69.
10 Erik H. Erikson, *Identity, Youth and Crisis* (New York: Faber and Faber Ltd, 1968), p. 18.

past, there has been too much emphasis placed on the 'crisis' part of this process, inviting adolescents to reject order and shun authority and quite possibly prompting parents and guardians to expect this rejection. I recall chatting with a parent who was bewildered that her son was doing well in school, playing an active role in the soccer club and frequently enjoyed chatting with his younger siblings. She was bracing herself for the crisis and wondering if it was worse when delayed. Personally, I have worked with many adolescents in whom no such crisis ever emerged.

By moving into formal operational thought, a teenager lets go of a concrete way of thinking and begins to engage with life in a more analytical and critically reflective way. In terms of religion this engagement leads to a letting go of parental values and launching out on a journey to invest time and energy in a set of independently owned values. According to Steinberg, a well-known American psychology professor, an adolescent who continues to conform to his or her parents' religious beliefs without ever questioning them or trying to embrace them as his or her own may well be showing signs of 'immature conformity' as opposed to spiritual maturity.[11] It takes a long time to form and shape an identity and the development of religious thinking is better understood as part of the overall structure. Exploring the mental, moral and spiritual challenges that are part of an adolescent's identity formation has proved hugely instrumental in our choice of school for our adolescent boys.

Faith Development Theory

James Fowler, a professor of theology and human development, formulated a faith development theory that people move through six stages as their faith matures, which can be applied not only to traditional faiths but to every manner of religion and belief. Fowler's

11 Laurence Steinberg, *Adolescence*, sixth international edition (New York: McGraw-Hill Higher Education, 2002).

theory describes faith not as a specific religion or a set of beliefs but as 'interactive and social' and a 'human universal concern', embedded in the 'shared visions and values that hold human groups together'.[12] As a Catholic parent I interpret this theory as one that integrates my faith and spirituality, thus manifesting itself in my lived reality in both a personal and communal way. Many people describe their faith as being of a 'private nature', yet one may suggest that it is necessary to find ways of establishing that Christian faith, by its very essence, cannot be a private affair:

> A new command I give you: Love one another. As I have loved you, so you must love one another. By this everyone will know that you are my disciples, if you love one another. (Jn 13:34-35)

In order to follow in his footsteps, it is necessary to ascertain that at the outset of his ministry Jesus called together a community of disciples (Mt 4:18-22). Maria Harris eloquently stated that 'to be, is to be with', and that a Christian's being in the world, made in the image and likeness of God, thrusts that person into community with self, others and God.[13] In *Deus Caritas Est* Benedict XVI reminds us that 'Seeing with the eyes of Christ, I can give to others much more than their outward necessities; I can give them the look of love which they crave.'[14] Faith is much more powerful then than belief in a set of doctrines or a creed; it is understood as the core value system that is embraced by the heart and illuminates the process of growth in every human. Faith, as Fowler indicates, 'gives form and content to our imagining of an ultimate environment'.[15] For Christians this

---

12 Fowler, *Stages of Faith*, p. 5.

13 Maria Harris and Gabriel Moran, *Reshaping Religious Education: Conversations on Contemporary Practice* (Louisville, Kentucky: Westminster John Knox Press, 1998), p. 109.

14 Benedict XVI, *Deus Caritas Est*, God is Love (25 December 2005), n. 18.

15 Fowler, *Stages of Faith*, p. 8.

'ultimate environment' can be named as the kingdom of God (Lk 17:21).

Religious Identity

If the adolescent begins to shape a new adult identity, there are many facets that contribute to its final reality. One of these facets is whether a religious identity will emerge or not. My husband and I are all too aware that we are our children's primary educators, and this can be an overwhelming responsibility. We work hard to parent and provide role models for them, supporting and guiding them on how to be decent citizens and respectful beings in the world. We practice our faith, inviting and encouraging as we go. We need support though, and we've found this support in Catholic schools. As a mother and religious educator I have often noted that young people develop keener appreciation of their own faith story as they explore and learn about the other religions of the world. Therefore, it is suggested that being part of a community of faith in school, as well as at home and in the local parish, complements our hope that they will activate their innate spirituality and develop a personal relationship with Jesus Christ as well as a communal relationship with fellow Christians. In a climate of increased secularism, developing a religious identity is in many ways a counter-cultural experience, so being in a environment where others are working to develop their religiosity can only serve to support an adolescent in his or her search for meaning that finds its expression in religion.

Faith in the Real World

My younger son, who has an angelic little face, told me that he had found a great YouTube video that was religious in nature. I was overwhelmed with love and pride that this young teen felt able to share his insight with his mother. Alas my gushings were slightly misplaced as the video he showed me turned out to be ridiculing the faith that I had set my heart upon. He chuckled away as he showed me a video of pictures of Jesus popping up all over the place. He thought it was funny, I thought it mocked the omnipresence of God. I explained what I did not like about the message and that I thought it was bordering on offensive. He understood but still insisted that it was funny. In the end, we agreed to differ. Later, I reflected on the name of the video, which was something like 'The Irritating Jesus' and I mused that, in fact, accepting Jesus as part of your life could be pretty irritating sometimes. We are called to be loving, caring, meek and humble of heart, to be peacemakers, givers and sharers of the Good News. Sometimes it is hard to fulfil some or even any of these tasks; sometimes ego, pride, ignorance or even tired humanity gets in the way.

My older son, who is in mid-to-late adolescence, is now developing a meaningful spirituality that began with his own enquiring mind. An example of this type of enquiry came on an evening after a double science class. 'What if,' he said, 'Jesus was an alien and all the raising up into the sky and white smoke and stuff was a spaceship, the engines roaring. Just think, could that be possible? What if Jesus is from another planet and his father, God, made him look like us so that we wouldn't be afraid of him and he is trying to show us the way to live and how to love each other.' I was both fascinated and totally taken aback. This discussion came about at the end of the day and I had neither the energy nor the inclination to get involved. Yet the concept was so far away from what I would ever have imagined as an adolescent that I felt it important to talk it through. I recognised that he was seeking clarity on the divinity of Jesus, using the frame of reference available to him, and that it was crucial to allow him express his thoughts without judgement and to engage with them.

I offer these examples by way of explaining the reality of young people's experience of engaging with faith in the twenty-first century.

When talking about faith, Daniel O'Leary asks us to begin with the heart – not the heart of the other, but our own heart.[16] This advice constantly offers me direction as a parent. We have encouraged our children to question, to seek to open their minds and learn about and be respectful of other religions and worldviews. Yet I sometimes wonder if we are ready to deal with this emerging thought in our faith. Would it be easier if our kids did not ask awkward questions or present such experiences? On the other hand, I hold that it is entirely appropriate and necessary that parents and guardians take an active role in nurturing the beliefs they chose for their child at the baptismal font. Although engaging in discussions like those outlined above takes time, patience and perhaps some personal searching, it is to be encouraged in families. We offer our offspring the space to search for meaning in life, but they are journeying with us, their small boats are not rudderless, they are attached (on many different levels) to the mothership. I suggest, with respect, that for a parent who is trying to encourage a sense of spirituality and an owned faith in an adolescent, it is vital to journey through the seeking with the seeker.

Belonging

Achieving a sense of belonging in a community is both productive and life affirming at any stage during an individual's life. Given that it is a time of identity reshaping and restructuring, achieving a sense of belonging may be especially life affirming during adolescence. I truly believe that when our sons hear our sentiments of faith echoed in the classroom, gym, canteen or principal's office, those sentiments become rooted in a firmer and more meaningful way: they take on the mantle of truth. In a Catholic community one of the key concepts is solidarity and advocacy, thus a sense of belonging is never an added bonus, it is the bedrock of all experience. To spend the best part of

16 Daniel O'Leary, *Begin With the Heart: Recovering a Sacramental Vision* (Dublin: Columba Press, 2009).

the day in an environment that supports one's creativity, celebrates one's achievable ability and invites one to reach out to others in faith, hope and love is an environment that promotes growth in one's innate spirituality and thus a sense of belonging that has the ability to be sustained throughout a lifetime.

Belonging to a club, group or community gives a shared sense of identity and enhances self-esteem. As mentioned above, the framing of students' faith in a school community is hugely supportive to any parent or guardian who promotes a lived faith at home. Michael Hryniuk holds that if adolescents are afforded an opportunity to explore their spirituality and faith tradition together with the chance to engage in social justice, this coupling 'has the potential to respond to the deepest needs of young persons for meaning, belonging, and a sense of religious identity'.[17] Irish schools are magnificent in their tireless work for social justice and equality and Catholic schools add the spirituality of the action, engaging with the faith story of the tradition and tapping into innate spirituality. A sense of belonging and connectedness may act as a catalyst in the forming of a sense of identity. To feel that one belongs in a particular school is one thing; to feel that one belongs in the connectedness of the school's faith environment is another.

In *Youth 2K*, a body of research on adolescent faith in Ireland at the end of the twentieth century, David Tuohy and Penny Cairns considered that many Irish teenagers feel they have not yet been afforded the opportunity to activate their full membership of the Church; they articulate a desire to have an identity and a sense of belonging to a faith community, but do not see an obvious space or role where this can be achieved.[18] This research further contends

---

17 Michael Hryniuk, 'Creating a Space for God: Toward a Spirituality of Youth Ministry', *Religious Education* 100.2 (2005): pp. 139–56, p. 145.

18 David Tuohy and Penny Cairns, *Youth 2K: Threat or Promise to a Religious Culture?* (Dublin: Marino Institute of Education, 2000).

that adolescents find personal experience and the opportunity to participate deeply valuable. In light of this there has been a great surge of programmes and possibilities, both in the parish and in schools, for young people. Together with participative roles in liturgy and social justice work, Catholic post-primary schools offer programmes that promote and provide participative and meaningful roles for adolescents who wish to activate their adult faith. Programmes such as Faith Friends, Ember Leadership, Meitheal and the Pope John Paul II Award exist to support adolescents in their choice to live in accordance with gospel values and in an effort to enrich faith. It is a basic tenet of education that we learn by doing. Adolescents especially become animated and empowered by action for justice, prayer that is rooted in their daily lives and efforts, participative relationships and leadership roles. All of the above programmes encourage, enlighten and engage adolescents in their search for meaning, and as programmes that are grounded in faith they support this search for meaning to find significant expression in religion.

Conclusion

Catholic schools themselves have always been person-centred, with an emphasis on the dignity of that person. Kath Engebretson's research on the teenage spirituality of boys explains that to activate the spiritual aptitude of an adolescent it is necessary to ignite the imagination.[19] In my experience, the imagination can be stirred through art, music, science and so much more. One might suggest that it can also be stirred and sealed with the breath of the Holy Spirit in prayer, in relationship with self, others and God by taking a sacramental view of life. Ensuring that reflective space and retreat time is built into the annual schedule is a reality within a Catholic school.

19 Kath Engebretson, 'Teenage Boys, Spirituality and Religion', *International Journal of Children's Spirituality* 9.3 (2004): pp. 263–78.

Quite recently I heard one of the priests from the community where our sons go to school speaking at Mass. He mused on the parable of the sower, as I myself have many times. This parable has always challenged me as I felt that it was a tad obvious the seeds would flourish on fertile soil and not on the path, the thorns or the rocks. However, it was at this celebration that I gained incredible clarity. The celebrant asked a local farmer, 'Why do you think there is no grass seed taking root this spring?' 'Because the ground temperature is too low for it to root,' replied the farmer. 'In order for the grass seed to grow, the ground must be between six and seven degrees at night, and the temperatures are not rising. The ground must have a pulse for the grass to grow.' The priest spoke about this wonderful analogy: a pulse in the earth. The Good News will fall on deaf ears if there is no pulse of reception to encourage it to take root. It is in a Catholic school that this pulse can be nurtured. The rhythm of the pulse initiated by parents, guardians and grandparents can be sustained, and the ability to keep that pulse alive to bear witness to the possibility of being fertile ground is celebrated.

Choosing a Catholic school for our children has been the right choice for us. They feel a huge sense of belonging, they are supported in their search for an identity and their search for meaning is afforded the opportunity to find its expression in our faith story. These years are formative and irreplaceable. We hope and pray that they become adults who can speak of their faith, own their beliefs and convictions and make every effort to live their call to be fully human and fully alive. Of course this is what all parents hope for their children. It takes energy and commitment and we stumble and fail daily, but we find rays of light and hope along the way. We chose a Catholic school because it continues our cherishing during the day. This is valued added in terms of our children's education. Together with formation as responsible citizens they are working from the same faith perspective as their parents. This encourages our hope. We are an Easter people.

A Visit to the Heart of Catholic Education: The Diocesan Advisor's Perspective on the Primary Classroom and Beyond

John-Paul Sheridan

For the last sixteen years I have been the diocesan advisor for Primary School Catechetics in the Diocese of Ferns. There is an advisor in every diocese in Ireland, who spends a certain amount of time visiting primary schools during the academic year. To define the role is not an easy one, and it can differ from diocese to diocese, but visiting classes is one of the most important parts of the role, and it is certainly one of the most enjoyable. In the past, the role was seen as one of inspection – where the children were asked questions and the various classes in the school were graded according to the ability of the children. Often they were the old Catechism questions, which were learnt by rote and answered accordingly. These visits often coincided with the celebration of the sacraments in the parish. Older people have told me stories of the fear and tension that often preceded the visit of the diocesan inspector and the worry of not getting any questions asked of them right. We live in very different times today, and I am glad to say that my visit to a school no longer incites fear or anxiety.

Since the advent of the *Children of God* series and then the *Alive-O* programme, the role of the diocesan advisor has changed considerably. Most see themselves first as a support to the teachers, and second as a support to the faith life of both the classroom and the school in general. I still ask questions, because the children often like to tell me what they know and because it is a way of getting them to talk about what they have learnt: about the Bible story they have been hearing, a song they have been learning or something about the time of year it is – Lent, Advent and so on. Depending on the time available, I will suggest that they ask me questions in return. This provides a great opportunity to engage with the children and sometimes, in a situation where the local priest doesn't call to the school that often, an opportunity to let them ask questions about the priesthood – about what it is like not to be married, if I have brothers and sisters, what my favourite thing about being a priest is, and so on. The children usually have a song prepared, which they will sing before the end of a visit, and we might also end with a prayer.

Visits prior to the reception of the sacraments of First Reconciliation, First Holy Communion and Confirmation will focus on what the children have been learning in preparation – the prayers, the various aspects of the sacraments and some of the music. Again, I am not there to check up on the teacher, but perhaps to assist where I might see a lack of something, to offer a refocus if the preparation is unbalanced, as well as a proffering of various resources that I have accumulated over the years. The teachers in the diocese of Ferns are hard-working, committed professionals with a genuine interest in and care for their pupils, and a desire to educate and prepare them to the best of their considerable ability. In the last number of years I have formed a team of retired primary teachers who visit the schools with me. This means that all classes are visited during a call to a school and not just the sacramental classes. The schools in the diocese, which number nearly one hundred, are now well-used to the team coming to the school, and the team forms a valuable and appreciated part of the diocesan work of education. Furthermore, as teachers themselves, they know and understand the difficulties and challenges in teaching a religious education programme. Many other dioceses have similar teams made up of lay people who contribute greatly to the work of primary religious education and catechesis in Ireland.

My years as advisor have given me a very real insight into the primary schools in my diocese and a keen awareness of the nature of Catholicism in Ireland today. My intention here is to offer some thoughts on the Catholic primary school as I have found it, in and of itself but also in the wider spheres of family and home and parish and community. It is not my intention to suggest that the Catholic school is better than any other patronage model, but to show what lies at the heart of the idea of the Catholic primary school, and how the schools that I have experienced over my year as a diocesan advisor are living and thriving witnesses to the gospel, which is at the core of every Christian endeavour.

The Changing Landscape

The past sixteen years have seen so much change in this country as to make it almost unrecognisable to previous generations. While this is not the place to chronicle all such shifts, I would like to mention three changes that have a relevance to the topic at hand.

From the point of view of religious education and the job of handing on the faith, it becomes increasingly difficult to compete in a milieu saturated with symbols and brands, consumables and the materialistic when we seek to lead the child to the transcendent and to a different set of symbols and values. Richard Louv's words, written twenty years ago on the life of the American child, have a resonance with children in Ireland at present:

> Today's children are living a childhood of firsts. They are the first day-care generation; the first truly multi-cultural generation; the first generation to grow up in the electronic bubble, the environment defined by computers and formed by television; the first post-sexual revolution generation; the first generation for which nature is more abstraction than reality; the first generation to grow up in new kinds of dispersed, deconcentrated cities, not quite urban, rural, or suburban.
>
> The combined force of these changes produces a seemingly unstoppable dynamic process: childhood today is defined by the expansion of experience and the contraction of positive adult contact. Each part of this process feeds and speeds the other. The more of the manmade world that children experience, the more they assume they know (and as they become teenagers, the less they think they need adults). Because children seem to know more about the world, adults are more likely to assume, sometimes wishfully, that kids can take care of themselves.[1]

Irish society has changed considerably both in terms of its makeup, its economic situation and in its attitude to religion:

> Being Catholic no longer permeates everyday life as it did a generation ago. To what extent are young Catholics being taught to say Catholic prayers and engage in Catholic rituals? To what extent has there been a decline in religious iconography, particularly the display of holy pictures and statues? In becoming less involved in the institutional Church, Irish Catholics have become more like their counterparts elsewhere in Europe. In

---

1 Richard Louv, *Childhood's Future* (San Diego: Anchor Books, 1990), pp. 5–6.

so far as they see themselves as belonging to a religious heritage without embodying institutional beliefs and practices, they are becoming more like their Protestant counterparts.[2]

Finally, there have been considerable changes in Irish education and in the primary school. Some changes have been quick and sudden, others slower and less obvious. The period of economic prosperity brought a great deal of investment in education, both in terms of new school buildings and classrooms, and in the provision of special needs assistants, remedial teachers and other assistance to the educational life of the child. It brought new children to the classrooms, some who didn't speak much or any English. It brought different faiths to schools and different and diverse cultures, as mentioned by former president Mary McAleese:

> Our population is growing, new neighbourhoods of strangers are springing up, and immigrants bring with them different cultures and embrace the richness of ours, as I have observed in the schools where their children speak to me proudly in Irish.[3]

This period of change also brought about new models of school patronage and questions regarding the provision of so many Catholic schools. In its 2007 document, *Catholic Primary School: A Policy for Provision into the Future*, the Irish Bishops stated that: 'the Catholic Church upholds the primacy of parents' rights in the education of their children', but that 'Catholic parents have also the duty and the right to choose schools that can best promote the Catholic education

---

2   Tom Inglis, 'Catholic Identity in Contemporary Ireland: Belief and Belonging to Tradition', *Journal of Contemporary Religion* 22.2 (2007): pp. 205–20, pp. 217–8.

3   Mary McAleese, Second Inaugural Speech (2004), http://www.president.ie.

of their children'.[4] It is on this basis that much of the debate on the role of the Catholic Church in education has hinged. The Council for Research and Development of the Irish Episcopal Conference's research in 2011 into *Parental Understandings of School Patronage* showed that parents' 'own memories of religious socialisation and formation in school often provide the template against which their child's experience is compared. This arises because there is not an intimate knowledge of the current RE programme operated in Catholic schools.'[5]

It is all too easy for anyone to view the work of schools within the narrow definition of academic excellence. As Bishop Leo O'Reilly stated:

The Church has a vital role to play in keeping alive, promoting and exemplifying commitment to education as a value in itself. Education in a secular, consumer society is always in danger of becoming a product, a commodity. In the era of the rise and fall of the Celtic Tiger it is difficult to resist the consumer model of education focused primarily on the service of the economy. The emphasis tends to be on competition and there is often a narrow focus on academic and easily measurable results.[6]

On a darker note, the last number of years has also brought revelations regarding sexual and institutional abuse and, as a result, questions have been raised as to whether the Catholic Church should play any role at all in education. However the Council of Europe recognises the significant part religious education plays in the school life of the child, stating that:

4 Irish Espiscopal Conference, *Catholic Primary School: A Policy for Provision into the Future* (Dublin: Veritas, 2007), 1.1; 1.2.

5 Irish Episcopal Conference, *Parental Understandings of School Patronage* (Maynooth, Co. Kildare: Council for Research and Development, 2011).

6 Leo O'Reilly, *Catholic Primary Education: Facing New Challenges*, Eugene Duffy, ed. (Dublin: Columba Press, 2012), p. 136.

» Religion is an important cultural fact (similar to other identity sources such as languages, history or cultural heritage).

» Beliefs about the world and values must be developed gradually, based on real personal and social learning experiences.

» An integrated approach to spiritual, religious, moral and civic values must be encouraged.[7]

Important though this is, it is only half the picture. The work of the Catholic school cannot be limited to just teaching religion as 'an important cultural fact', but must go further and help to shape and develop the spiritual life of the pupil.

The Catholic School

The Declaration on Christian Education from the Second Vatican Council, *Gravissimum Educationis*, states that the proper function of the Catholic school is to 'create for the school community a special atmosphere animated by the gospel spirit of freedom and charity' (GE, n. 8). Many of the other Church documents regarding Catholic schools and education emphasise this:

Catholic schools must be seen as meeting places for those who wish to express Christian values in education. The Catholic school, far more than any other, must be a community whose aim is the transmission of values for living. Its work is seen as promoting a faith-relationship with Christ in whom all values find fulfilment. But faith is principally assimilated through contact with people whose daily life bears witness to it. Christian faith, in fact, is born and grows inside a community.[8]

---

7 Council of Europe, *Religious Diversity and Intercultural Education: A Reference Book for Schools* (Strasbourg: Publishing Division, Directorate of Communications, 2006), p. 7.

8 Sacred Congregation for Catholic Education, *The Catholic School* (19 March 1977), n. 53, www.vatican.va.

Why Send Your Child To A Catholic School?

From the moment a diocesan advisor walks through the doors of the primary school, there is evidence of this 'community of faith'. It is not just apparent in the Christian symbols on the walls or the sacred space in the corridor denoting the particular season of the liturgical year, it can be seen through the artwork of the children on the walls, the notices showing the 'pupil of the week' and the school and pupils' achievements. All these for me are signs of a school that is fulfilling its part in the 'salvific mission of the Church' because it is 'precisely in the gospel of Christ, taking root in the minds and lives of the faithful, that the Catholic school finds its definition'.[9] For me the part of the gospel being fulfilled here is Christ's message to cherish the children, to whom the kingdom of God belongs (Mt 19:14; Mk 10:13-16). This is suggested in the *Religious Dimension of Education in a Catholic School*:

> In a Catholic school, everyone should be aware of the living presence of Jesus 'the Master' who, today as always, is with us in our journey through life as the one genuine 'teacher' ... the gospel spirit should be evident in a Christian way of thought and life which permeates all facets of the educational climate.[10]

However it might be said that every primary school, regardless of patronage, cherishes its pupils and makes their school a welcoming and happy community. As *Catholic Primary Schools: A Policy for Provision into the Future* states, 'What distinguishes the Catholic school is that its concept of the human person is rooted in the teaching of Jesus Christ as embodied in the Catholic faith community.'[11] And according to the *General Directory for Catechesis*, it is 'the special function' of the Catholic school to:

---

9   Ibid., n. 9.
10 Sacred Congregation for Catholic Education, *The Religious Dimension of Education in a Catholic School* (1988), p. 26.
11 *Catholic Primary School: A Policy for Provision into the Future*, 4.1.

» develop in the school community an atmosphere animated by a spirit of liberty and charity.

» enable young people, while developing their own personality, to grow at the same time in that new life which has been given to them in Baptism.

» orientate the whole of human culture to the message of salvation.[12]

This notion of community is at the heart of the Christian family and at the heart of the primary school is inclusive of all – teacher, pupils, classroom assistants, auxiliary staff, local clergy and school chaplains, as well as boards of management, parents councils and individual parents.

Partners in Education

All these Church documents see parents as the primary educators of their child. Parents have taken the first step to baptise their child, and then subsequent steps as they begin to teach their child to pray, how to bless themselves and how to behave. For children it is the 'first explicit experience and practice of the faith'.[13] Parents then take the next step to send them to a Catholic school, where that work is continued under the care of teachers and an entire school community whose role in Catholic education is two-fold: 'its service in the mission of the Church and its service to society'.[14] The philosopher Santayana stated that 'a child educated only at school is an uneducated child'. I would hope that this is the case for religious education also – that the work of religious education is begun long before the child starts school, and that when the child enters the school we begin a work of collaboration:

---

12 Sacred Congregation for the Clergy, *General Directory for Catechesis* (1997), p. 259.

13 Ibid., p. 178.

14 *Catholic Primary School: A Policy for Provision into the Future*, 3.3.

Beginning school means, for the child, entering a society wider than the family, with the possibility of greater development of intellectual, affective and behavioural capacities. Often specific religious instruction will be given in school. All this requires that catechesis and catechists constantly co-operate with parents and school teachers as suitable opportunities arise. Pastors should remember that, in helping parents and educators to fulfil their mission well, it is the Church who is being built up.[15]

After home and school, the third location for religious education is the parish:

In many parts of Ireland the community of the parish continues to act as a centre of Catholic religious education, worship and liturgical celebration for those whom it serves. The great strength of the Catholic primary school system in Ireland has been its rootedness in parish communities, where the school commands the support and loyalty of the families involved. The primary school is an integral part of the local community in many areas and itself plays a unique role in community building. It provides a focus where families meet and get to know each other, and around which they are united by a shared interest in the welfare of their children. It gives the local community a sense of ownership of the educational enterprise and a corresponding commitment to ensure that the enterprise flourishes and succeeds.[16]

The home, school and parish form what is commonly referred to as the 'three-legged stool' of religious education. Another way of looking

---

15 *General Directory for Catechesis*, p. 179.
16 Irish Episcopal Conference, *Vision '08: A Vision for Catholic Education in Ireland* (Dublin: Veritas, 2008).

at this dynamic is in terms of what is called religious socialisation, which might be defined as 'the transmission and internalisation of societal values and norms'.[17] It is impossible to sit on a three-legged stool if any of its legs are missing. Therefore, religious education in the home is as important as that taught in church and school in the faith development of a child.

The Spiritual Life of the Child

> Can [children] have a genuine relationship with God? Here are the responses of two eight-year-olds to the question, 'Have you ever felt God close to you?' 'Yah. Um, it sounds pretty silly, but when I'm lying in bed, my covers are his arms and my pillow was his chest. I feel like he's around me.' 'It feels like someone's just sitting by you. And it's nice to know that it's Jesus, or God.' Those who work with children are often moved by such beautiful expressions of a child's joy or peace in God's presence.[18]

Sometimes children have the ability to articulate their understanding of God in an uncomplicated manner, a talent that sadly many adults fail to hold on to. This raw sense of the presence of God is something that is nurtured and developed during religious education. I have yet to meet a child who is not enthused by the religious education in the classroom. I am constantly encouraged by the sacramental preparation that is undertaken by the pupils under the guidance of creative and motivated teachers. One could be cynical about the pupils' motivation coming up to First Holy Communion and

---

17 Paul Vermeer, 'Religious Education and Socialization', *Religious Education* 105.1 (2010): pp. 103–16, p. 104.
18 Scottie May, Beth Posterski, Catherine Stonehouse and Linda Cannell, *Children Matter: Celebrating Their Place in the Church, Family, and Community* (Grand Rapids, MI: Eerdmans, 2005), p. 48.

Confirmation, but discussion with teachers will usually set the worst of cynics right. It is not always about the money, the clothes and the day out. I am often profoundly struck by some of the answers that the children give, by the care they take with classmates with special needs and by the candour and sense of fun that is sometimes engendered during their religion lessons. This is not just the wonderful work of teachers and parents, but it is the work of the Holy Spirit in the life and mind of the child. It is the work of spiritual formation, the goal of which might be defined as 'a maturing faith and a deepening relationship with Jesus Christ, through which we become more like Christ in the living of our everyday lives in the world'.[19]

Regarding what we 'do' in school in terms of religious education, the introduction to the *Alive-O* programme, which is used in Catholic primary schools in Ireland, states:

> The kind of knowing that we seek is not only one which leads to clarity of thought and articulation … We seek to lead the children to become the kind of people who see the world around them and all that is happening in it through the eyes of faith, and whose interpretations of what is happening and responses to it are all influenced by their faith. Religious education must lead children to respond to God here and now with faith, love and gratitude. Therefore, we must communicate the Christian message to them in a manner appropriate to their age, stage of faith development and life experience. The entire programme is profoundly biblical, in the sense that it presents God as a living God who is present and active in our daily lives. Through the programme we help the children to relate their discovery of themselves, of other people and of the world, to

---

19 Catherine Stonehouse, *Joining Children on the Spiritual Journey: Nurturing a Life of Faith* (Grand Rapids, MI: Baker Books, 1998), p. 21.

God who is the creator of all things, the source of all life, who loves and cares for each of them and is always with them.[20]

This is how the children in primary schools begin to develop an idea of what it means to be a child of God. In a gradual and progressive manner over the course of their primary education the child is introduced to the truths of our Catholic faith and tradition. This is done in a manner that resonates with their young age and faith development. We begin slowly and gradually to move through the stories and prayers, the songs and the season, the artwork and the writing until they are prepared for the sacraments. It is not work that is undertaken only during time specifically set aside for religious education. It is taught in a manner that integrates it with the other subjects in the school day, so that it doesn't become merely one among many subjects, but the subject that calls to the heart and soul of the child.

In the area of religious faith, it is not just what we know, but how we respond to that knowledge, and put that knowledge into practice. This is usually called catechesis, coming from the Greek *katekhesis*, meaning 'to echo'. It is neither advisable nor necessary to separate these two elements, and both are attended to in the course of the school day. Take, for example, the story of the Good Shepherd. It is important that the child hears about this parable of Jesus. The shepherd goes to look for the sheep that is lost, finds it and brings it home. It is also important that the child sees the connection between the shepherd who looks for the lost sheep and Jesus who is the good shepherd, who is constantly looking for us when we stray and get lost. The child learns the information, but then takes that information and uses it as part of the preparation for First Reconciliation, learning to understand, through prayer, song and reflection that the Good

20 Irish Episcopal Commission on Catechetics, *Alive-O 4: Religious Education Programme for Second Class/Primary Four Teachers' Book* (Dublin: Veritas, 1999), p. xi.

Shepherd is the one who forgives us, who finds us and brings us home. In other words, in the Catholic school while we are *informing* the child, we are also *forming* the child in the faith.

The Spiritual Life of the School

The curriculum of a school seeks to help the child develop the skills necessary in life, and the curriculum in the area of religious education is also about teaching and forming the child in the skills and dispositions necessary to be part of the Christian family. Over time, methods have changed, but the core *raison d'être* of the curriculum is still much the same:

> Mindful of the fact that the human being has been redeemed by Christ, the Catholic school aims at forming in the Christian those particular virtues which will enable them to live a new life in Christ and help them to play faithfully their part in building up the kingdom of God.[21]

That a school should be seen less as an institution and more as a community gives a clear insight into what might be called 'the vocation of the school', which might be described as follows:

> Primary schools are dynamic places where children learn about themselves and the world they live in. They make friends, form relationships and are provided with the tools to learn. One of the things that children learn, in schools with a religious patron, is an understanding of God. This understanding is informed by the ethos of that school. In this sense, schools are places where a child's faith is fostered and developed.[22]

---

21 Sacred Congregation for Catholic Education, *The Catholic School* (1977), p. 36.
22 Irish Episcopal Conference, *Parental Understandings of School Patronage* (Maynooth, Co. Kildare: Council for Research and Development, 2011), p. 3.

In any family, there is a sense of a common purpose – to celebrate on the big occasions of life; to be a source of strength and mutual support at moments of sorrow; to teach the next generation and bring them up to the best of the family's ability; to share the history and story of the family. It is essentially the same in any Christian community and it is the same in the community of the school. For me the easiest way to be reminded of this is to be a regular visitor to the schools in my diocese. We need to go back to that 'perfect' early Christian community to understand what I'm talking about:

> And they devoted themselves to the apostles' teaching and fellowship, to the breaking of bread and the prayers. And all who believed were together and had all things in common; and they sold their possessions and goods and distributed them to all, as any had need. And day by day, attending the temple together and breaking bread in their homes, they partook of food with glad and generous hearts, praising God and having favour with all the people. And the Lord added to their number day by day those who were being saved. (Acts 2:42, 44-47)

This section of the Acts of the Apostles gives an indication as to how this early community of Jesus' followers conducted themselves, leading the writer Tertullian to say, 'See the Christians, see how they love each other'. What we nurture in the Catholic school is something of this early community.

The apostles' teaching might be suggested as the content of the religious education classes at each level. As mentioned already, during the primary school years we seek to nurture the gift of faith given to children at baptism, by opening to them the mysteries of their faith, by teaching them about the person of Jesus and how they act towards one another in a manner that follows what Jesus asked. One might be forgiven for thinking that this is where the work of the

Catholic school begins and ends. It is not. What the community of the Catholic school is concerned with are the other elements of that early Christian community.

The children learn about the 'breaking of bread' in terms of their sacramental preparation, both for First Holy Communion and also in regard to the celebration of other sacraments in the life of the Christian community. However, they also learn about the idea of celebration and how it is shared on occasions in the life of the school: birthdays and anniversaries; winning competitions and sports events; communal meals and sharing food. They also come to understand the wider context of learning to share with those less fortunate than themselves: at Lent with the Trócaire collections; collecting for local and national charities and awareness of the wider global family with whom we have an obligation to 'break bread'.

While learning prayers is important in the faith life of the child, I have experienced schools' regular celebrations of assemblies and school Masses. Prayer becomes the pulse of the school day, from morning prayers and assemblies to the Angelus, prayers before and after meals and prayers before going home. Often this is augmented by small, simple rituals in the class, and complimented by the classroom or school's sacred space, where there is a visual representation of the seasons of the liturgical year, giving the children a reminder every time they see it.

In the last few years some schools have been experimenting with meditation and mindfulness, giving over a small portion of the week to simple meditation. Every class takes part, and teachers have reported how well the children have responded. Prayer, as with many of the areas of the religious education curriculum, is not just about giving children a certain quantity of knowledge but hopefully equipping them for the future, when they might seek its comfort in the face of adversity and will have the ability to know how to address their deepest hearts' desires to their heavenly Father. Einstein suggested that 'education is what remains after one has forgotten what one has learned in school'. How a Catholic school forms the spiritual life of the child is very much about what is left, even after lessons are forgotten.

For children in crisis, the school can often be one of the few places of stability and refuge. None of the various models of school patronage have a monopoly on this. In the Catholic school, we do it in a particular way and for a particular reason. Pope Benedict XVI mentioned the passage from Acts in his first encyclical *Deus Caritas Est* (God is Love). He showed that this early Christian community was about the mission of love:

> Love of neighbour, grounded in the love of God, is first and foremost a responsibility for each individual member of the faithful, but it is also a responsibility for the entire ecclesial community at every level: from the local community to the particular Church and to the Church universal in its entirety. As a community, the Church must practice love.[23]

As a Christian community, we are in the business of love, and it is likewise with the school community. A school that understands its vocation as a community, building up the body of Christ and being a living, tangible sign of the kingdom of God, is a school community that is grounded in love of God and love of neighbour.

'Language' and Religious Education

The word I prefer to use when speaking about faith is 'language'. When a child begins in school they are introduced to the language of the school. This means that things are done in a certain way: teachers are addressed in a certain way, the children play in certain yards and they have a certain timetable to follow. They must ask permission,

---

23 Benedict XVI, *Deus Caritas Est* (2006), n. 20.

and must put up their hand; they learn to play together and learn to share. It is the socialisation of the child into the community of the school. Some children arrive at school already equipped with many of these skills, especially if they have been to playschool, or come from a family with brothers and sisters. Many teachers will say that this language works best when there is support from the home, where a similar language of discipline, regularity and order is spoken – manners, chores, bed at specific times, and so on.

When it comes to religious education, there is a language that the children begin to learn in Junior Infants. It is the language of symbols and signs, where the children are initiated into the rich semiology and symbology which is part of the Christian tradition. It is the language of gathering and ritual, through which the children learn to be part of the Christian community and how to play their part in the associated sacraments, rituals and spiritual life of the community. It is the language of word and story – children learn of the life of Jesus Christ and how to apply its message to their lives. They learn to speak words of peace and love, sorrow and thanksgiving, prayer and praise.

As with the language of the school, the language of faith is always best understood when the child recognises it as one spoken in other places – in the Church on a weekday or Sunday morning, in the homes of their relations, neighbours and friends, and most importantly, spoken by their parents or guardians and others at home. Consider this: how many times do you have to remind a child to say 'please' or 'thank you' before they do it voluntarily? Now, think how difficult it is to teach a child to bless themselves or to genuflect, when the only place it is being done is in the school or the classroom or during the occasional school visit to the church.

Picture the scene: your son or daughter arrives home from school and announces that they have been chosen to play for the school team in some major school league match. There is great enthusiasm and pride and you are delighted for your child. You promise to help them in all the preparation and hard work over the next few months. You drive him or her to training sessions and encourage them from the sideline. On the drive home and during countless family meals you talk about strategy and skill, encourage where there is room for improvement and offer suggestions for difficulties they are experiencing. You want to offer all the advice and knowledge you yourself learned in the past, and you praise them as their technique improves and their confidence grows. Your child's team wins the various matches in the league and eventually the final looms on the horizon. The day of the big match arrives and you get all your relatives and friends to attend. The school comes out in force and the local park is full with supporters from both sides. The game begins and your child is playing the best they ever have. You are so proud, especially when they score a few points and help lead the school team to a resounding victory. The final whistle blows and you are ecstatic. As the celebrations get under way you are approached by the manager of the county team, who congratulates your child on their performance. His parting words are that if they continue to play like that, he'll be looking for them in a few years' time to play for the county. Eventually everything calms down and you head home for a big celebration. In the days following, your child puts their gear and the medal that they won into the back of the wardrobe and never plays again. All that training, all that skill, all that potential wasted.

It may seem frivolous to equate a sports event with the seriousness of the sacraments of First Holy Communion or Confirmation, but I think the analogy is comparable to what I see as in my role in diocesan advisor. On visits to schools prior to Confirmation I am struck by the dedication and enthusiasm of the children that are preparing for the sacrament. I'm hopeful, thinking of the potential that might be realised for the future life of the Church. Yet sadly this potential too often goes unrealised. Confirmation becomes all about the big day and little else after that. It has been often called, rather cynically, the sacrament of exit: you make your confirmation and then leave the Church. Faith, commitment and everything else so earnestly studied and learned is forgotten or ignored, despite enthusiastic and dedicated teachers who, within the context of the living, visible and fruitful Christian community of the Catholic school, seek to enflame the hearts and souls of the pupils in their class.

Bressanone Speech

The story is told that the Pope Emeritus Benedict XVI used to meet groups of priests while on holidays in northern Italy and would have a question and answer session with them. One such encounter took place in the cathedral in Bressanone in August 2008. The Holy Father was asked by a parish priest about the situation of children presenting for the sacraments of First Holy Communion and Confirmation who fail to be part of the Sunday Eucharist. The pope's answer was a long one, but the final part is worth quoting:

> ... the pedagogy of faith is always a journey and we must accept today's situations. Yet, we must also open them more to each person, so that the result is not only an external memory of things that endures but that their hearts have truly been touched. The moment when we are convinced the heart is touched – it has felt a little of Jesus' love, it has felt a little the desire to move along these lines and in this direction. That is the moment when, it seems to me, we can say that we have made a true catechesis. The proper meaning of catechesis, in fact, must be this: to bring the flame of Jesus' love, even if it is a small one, to the hearts of children, and through the children to their parents, thus reopening the places of faith of our time.[24]

---

24 Benedict XVI, *Meeting of the Holy Father with the Clergy of the Diocese of Bolzano-Bressanone* (6 August 2008), www.vatican.va. Cited by Maeve Mahon and Martin Delaney in the sacramental preparation programme *Do This In Memory*.

The pope's answer is curious, because instead of laying the responsibility of 'handing on the faith' with the parent, he states that often when the light of faith is brought to the child, it can then move from the child to the parents. When the heart of a child is touched in the preparation and celebration of the sacraments of Initiation, then perhaps the parents' hearts will also be touched. In the context of the Catholic schools in Ireland at this time, the spiritual life of the child is awakened and nurtured, sustained and helped to grow. Sometimes it is done in collaboration with the parish and the home, sometimes not, but nonetheless it is done. When we celebrate the place of the Catholic school in our parishes and communities, we are celebrating one of 'the places of faith of our time'.

Finally, I refer to *Share the Good News*, which stated the following regarding the Catholic school:

> Primary schools seek to launch children on their lifelong journey with an education that honours them personally and helps them to develop and use their affective, active and cognitive learning capacities. Heart, hands and head all have a role to play in how we learn and what we learn. Religious education for children necessitates such a synthesis between heart, hands and head. At the same time, it contributes to ensuring that the education children receive is holistic, experiential and life-enhancing.[25]

During my years spent visiting the primary schools of Wexford and South Wicklow, I have experienced what is best about that vision for primary school and religious education: children being set along a path with the skills to conquer life, the disposition to enhance life and the intellect to interpret life. What Catholic primary schools do is give

---

25 *Share the Good News: The National Directory for Catechesis in Ireland* (Dublin: Veritas, 2010), p. 99.

children the understanding that Christ is not only the destination of that journey, but also their companion.

Learning How to Live: Offering Your Child the Gift of Catholic Religious Education

Anne Hession

It has been suggested that we have children because we want the good in our lives to continue.[1] In terms of the focus of this book this statement generates the question: what in your life do you wish could continue into the next generation? What way of living have you found to be true and worthwhile? The way we live our lives answers the deep 'spiritual' questions that all people inevitably face at some point in their lives. Is it good to be alive? Is human life the whole story or is there something which matters beyond life? Is the human being matter, spirit or both? Does life have a purpose or meaning? Is the person essentially an individual or is openness to others or to God an intrinsic part of personhood? Can I discover truth? Does it really matter what I commit myself to? What if I fail in life? What about evil, suffering and tragedy in life? Who or what guides my moral decisions, the kind of person I think I should be, and the kind of society I want to help create?

---

1 Klaus Mollenhauer, *Vergessene Zusammenhänge: Über Kultur und Erziehung* [*Forgotten Connections: On Culture and Education*] (München: Juventa, 1994), pp. 17–18.

Every school ultimately teaches something relatively consistent about the 'spiritual' questions outlined above. In other words, education, by its nature, enables children to search for a meaningful spirituality or philosophy of life. When you choose one school over another you are not just choosing one set of *ideas* that you approve of. Whether you are conscious of it or not, your child will be invited to *be* and to *live* in a certain way by that school. All schools invite children to adopt a particular way of life in company with others, just as all schools form children in certain values and beliefs and not others.[2] The spirituality or philosophy of life proposed by the Catholic school will suit your child:

... If you believe in God

For Catholics, God is the Mystery that lies at the heart of all that exists. God is the ultimate reality, the Lord of the whole of life, the foundation of all creation. To believe in God is to believe that the reason we exist is that we have been loved into being by God. God created us simply because he wants to be in loving relationship with people who can respond. Therefore, when you place your child in a Catholic school, you are confirming your belief that your child is loved absolutely: they have been created by God, with a unique destiny with God in heaven. Those who believe in God will want their children to learn that everything – themselves, their families, their friends, the created world, the farthest supernova – exists because it is loved absolutely. They will want them to see everything as rooted in and sustained by the love of God, whether that part of the world or human experience being studied is found in science, geography, history, mathematics,

---

2   John L. Elias, 'Ancient Philosophy and Religious Education: Education as Initiation into a Way of Life', *International Handbook of the Religious, Moral and Spiritual Dimensions in Education*, M. de Souza et al., eds (Dordrecht: Springer, 2006), p. 12.

literature or art.[3] They will want them to encounter the truth God has revealed to us, above all, God's revelation of Jesus as 'the Way, the Truth, and the Life'. Finally, they will want them to learn that life has meaning and purpose, that God is to be found at the core of their being, that they have a unique role to play in God's plan for the world, that God wishes them to live the fullest possible lives in the world and that their ultimate destiny is with God in heaven.

In the Catholic school the presence of God is assumed and teachers in the school will be guided by a set of values and goals which derive from faith in God. In contrast, the multidenominational (or common) school is based on a secular philosophy of education. Here a set of secular values guide the everyday work of the school and the kinds of relationships that are valued. Multidenominational schools cannot shape the beliefs or personal qualities of pupils 'in the light of any substantial or "comprehensive" view of the person or of life which is significantly controversial'. This is because the cultivation of particular religious or spiritual perspectives, and qualities of personhood may not be justifiable within the setting of such schools given 'the demand for educational forbearance from influence on matters on which there is no public agreement'.[4]

Believers in God will not be happy to confine their children's religion to one part of life, such as the home, or even to a curriculum time slot designated 'religious education' at school. To do so would deny God's existence as the God of the whole of their children's lives.

---

3   Michael Himes, 'Living Conversation: Higher Education in a Catholic Context', *Conversations on Jesuit Higher Education* 8 (Fall, 1995): pp. 22–3.

4   Hanan Alexander and Terence H. McLaughlin, 'Education in Religion and Spirituality, *The Blackwell Guide to the Philosophy of Education*, N. Blake, P. Smeyers, R. Smith and P. Standish, eds (Oxford: Blackwell, 2002), p. 364. Terence H. McLaughlin, 'Education of the Whole Child?', *Education, Spirituality and the Whole Child*, R. Best, ed. (London: Cassell, 1996). For reflections on the concept of a 'common school' see Terence H. McLaughlin, 'Liberalism, Education and the Common School', *Journal of Philosophy of Education* 29. 2 (1995): p. 241.

Further, it would deny that faith gives them a new way of seeing and understanding *everything* and *everyone* they encounter, and that this way of experiencing the world cannot be cordoned off into one part of the school day. A school which limits its goals to preparing children for employment, for membership of society, for citizenship and even for critical thought will always fall short of the best education in the believer's eyes. Only a school that prepares their children for all of life, both here and hereafter, will honour God's presence and love as the matrix in which they and their children live and breathe.

... If you believe that Jesus is the best model of how to live a human life

The hallmark of the Catholic school is this radical claim: God became incarnate in the life, death and destiny of a particular human being, Jesus of Nazareth. In other words the absolute mystery of God became a fully human being in Jesus. This has two direct implications for Christians. First, Christians believe that God has been and is even now encountered in or through Jesus Christ. Second, they also believe that the person of Jesus, the way he lived and his vision of life, is of absolute significance for understanding how to live a good human life. In other words, the person of Christ sheds light on all the questions outlined at the beginning of this chapter about living, suffering and dying, about the meaning and purpose of life, about relationships, ethical dilemmas and social responsibilities.

We know from scripture that Jesus devoted his ministry to healing and reconciling, to building up human persons, especially the poor and the downtrodden. He was 'a fiercely tender presence',[5] passionate and outspoken, compassionate and wise, a charismatic prophet, preacher, teacher and healer. When Jesus healed social outcasts, such as the ten lepers (Lk 17:11-14), the crippled woman (Lk 13:10-17) or

---

5   Catherine Mowry LaCugna, *God For Us* (New York: HarperSanFrancisco, 1991), p. 293.

the haemorrhaging woman (Lk 8:43-48), his action was a sign of the presence of God. Again, through the meals he shared with all those who followed him, Jesus revealed that in the kingdom of God there are no distinctions and hierarchies between male and female, rich and poor, Gentile and Jew. Indeed, his followers were mainly made up of those who were excluded and marginalised from society, including women. Jesus aroused these people to unconditional faith in God. He told the sinful woman, 'Your faith has saved you; go in peace' (Lk 7:50), teaching that God's Spirit did not impose itself upon them externally but transformed them from within. The God he revealed recreates everything – heart, mind and body – providing the strength for people to transform themselves and their world.[6]

The Catholic school offers Jesus Christ as a model to children, so that their education becomes an invitation to become more like Christ, to live their lives guided by his values, to enter into a relationship with Christ and to transform society in imitation of him. Precisely because God chose to become one of us, we discover that it is in our human lives that he is encountered: whatever enables us to reach the fullness of their humanity and to live the fullest possible lives in the world enables us to become divine. This is one reason why the Catholic school will always resist the narrowing of educational goals to the needs of the economy or the state. Instead, it will always insist on developing each and every aspect of children's lives (aesthetic, creative, critical, cultural, emotional, intellectual, moral, physical, political, social and spiritual), enabling them to develop their talents, their creativity, their freedom, their intellect and their spirit.

Clearly, the culture children are immersed in today offers a rival imagination of the nature of human life to that of Jesus. As Michael Warren explains:

---

6   Jon Sobrino, *Jesus the Liberator*, 2nd ed. (Maryknoll, New York: Orbis Books, 1998), p. 99.

in modern industrial and post-industrial societies ... the wider culture is based on understandings and values that run counter to a religious vision. These values run toward unfettered capitalism, strategies of domination to protect financial privilege, and an ethic of consumerism.

This is why formation in a counter-cultural understanding of the human person has become so important in our time, 'precisely in the face of the powerful formative structures found in wider social and cultural life'.[7] Similarly, John Hull notes that our market societies offer children a false spirituality which tells them that 'human life consists in having, not in being; it promises to transform [them] not through love but through power'.[8] This 'false spirituality' is radically challenged by Jesus who revealed that the way to life is not the way of consumption and power but the way of service, compassion and love.

... If you want your child to have a positive and strong sense of his/her own worth

The development of a sense of self is central to the educational journey of children, and the need to understand themselves at the deepest level may be the place where the Catholic school will contribute most to your children's education. Understanding ourselves is discerning what is of crucial importance to us and what gives our lives meaning. In the Catholic school, children will learn that the deepest core of their identity does not depend on achievements, on how they look and what they have, on their ability to participate in the latest cultural

---

7   Michael Warren, 'Religious Formation in the Context of Social Formation', Jeff Astley, Leslie Francis, eds, *Critical Perspectives on Christian Education* (Leominster, Herefordshire: Gracewing, Fowler Wright Books, 1994), pp. 202–9.

8   John Hull, 'Spiritual Development: Interpretations and Applications', http://www. johnmhull.biz/, pp. 4–5 [accessed 20 June 2013].

trends or even on their human rights enshrined in law. Instead, they are invited to consider that their dignity and worth derives from the fact that they have been created in the image and likeness of God, with an immortal soul, and are ultimately called to share in God's own life. This is why Catholic religious education begins by teaching children that God loves them prior to any action on their part. They are loved just as they are. God's love for them precedes everything and will be there even if everything else were to fail them. God calls them to be the unique person God has created them to be, and the scope of their existence is now and for eternity.

... If you believe in awakening your child to the spiritual and religious dimensions of his/her own life

One of the core assumptions of the Catholic school is that the child is naturally spiritual and religious. This means that the child has an innate capacity or natural potential for relationship with God. To say that the child is intrinsically religious is to claim that the person cannot fail to ask the deeper questions which can only be truly answered by reference to God. Pope Benedict XVI described this 'religious dimension of the person' as 'a fundamental openness to otherness and to the mystery that presides over every relationship and every encounter with human beings'.[9] This is the particular insight that religions bring to education, an idea powerfully articulated by Rabindranath Tagore, the Bengali poet and Hindu:

> Our teachers in ancient India realised the soul of man as something very great indeed. They saw no end to its dignity ... Any limited view of man would therefore be an incomplete view. He could not reach his finality as a mere Citizen or Patriot,

---

9 Pope Benedict XVI, 'Address of his Holiness Benedict XVI to the Catholic Religion Teachers' (Saturday, 25 April, 2009). Available at www.vatican.va.

for neither City nor Country, nor the bubble called the World could contain his eternal soul.[10]

The child enrolled in the Catholic school is understood as essentially spiritual or religious in this sense, irrespective of the actual faith conviction and religious affiliation, or lack of it, of the actual student concerned.[11] Catholic education is committed to enabling the child to become aware of this dimension of their life and invites them to develop it in conversation with an ancient and rich spiritual and religious tradition.

Children's natural capacity for the spiritual can either be obscured or enhanced by the culture they live in. That children are not being afforded the opportunity to develop their spiritual lives in societies such as ours is becoming a real concern.[12] This is because religion has been largely removed from the public to the private domain with the result that children are learning that the language of spirituality and religion is not really valued, and so they tend to hide it. In this context, the importance of the Catholic educational commitment to awakening children to the depths and the mystery of their spiritual and religious lives, and to offering children a rich religious vocabulary for the spiritual questions and experiences they have, cannot be over-emphasised.

---

10 Rabindranath Tagore, 'The Four Stages of Life', *The Religion of Man,* Jaroslav Pelikan, *The World Treasury of Modern Religious Thought* (London: Little, Brown and Co., 1990), p. 151.

11 Anne Hunt, 'The Essence of Education is Religious', *International Handbook of the Religious, Moral and Spiritual Dimensions in Education,* M. de Souza et al., eds (Dordrecht: Springer, 2006), p. 648.

12 For example, in one large-scale study, British researchers David Hay and Rebecca Nye found that spirituality is 'massively present in the lives of children'. However, they found that children's spirituality is hidden because of what they term 'a culturally constructed forgetfulness' which causes them to suppress their natural spirituality. David Hay and Rebecca Nye, *The Spirit of the Child* (London: Harper Collins, 1998), pp. vi, 20.

... If you want your child to develop a Christian spirituality

It has been suggested that good spiritual education will enable children to learn how to practice a particular spiritual way of life *and* to have an appreciative understanding of other spiritual paths.[13] In the Catholic school, children are enabled to develop a Christian spirituality by exploring a holistic vision for their lives and by learning a specific spiritual language and practice that enable them to embody that vision. It is precisely by being securely rooted in a rich Christian spirituality that they become persons capable of sharing and appreciating the religious and spiritual insights of people who are different from themselves.

Christian spirituality is following Jesus in the practice of the love of God and neighbour. It is rooted in the experience of a personal encounter with Jesus Christ. In the Catholic school children are taught how to live their lives in the Spirit of Jesus as they encounter him in prayer, in the Word of God, in the sacraments and in their own lives. They are taught that they have the capacity to transcend the self, by knowing and loving other persons, including God. They are helped to awaken their capacity for wonder and awe, for joy and connection; for perceiving their environment in a new way, for understanding their need of redemption, and for encountering the Mystery of God.

... If you want your child to be religiously literate

The Catholic school supports the religious education children receive when they engage in the spiritual and liturgical practices of Christian life at home and in the parish. One of the greatest contributions the Catholic school can make to children's religious education is to enable them to reach a critical understanding of their own religion.

---

13 Gabriel Moran, 'The Aims of Religious Education', *Reshaping Religious Education: Conversations on Contemporary Practice*, Maria Harris and Gabriel Moran (Louisvillle, Kentucky: Westminster/ John Knox Press, 1998), pp. 30, 39–41.

The Catholic tradition has a strong commitment to the place of reason in the process of coming to faith and is strongly opposed to indoctrination in any form. As Dermot Lane explains, 'the act of faith is always a free act and if it loses that freedom, or if coercion is brought to bear, then it is no longer faith but some form of ideology'.[14] Unfortunately Catholic schools have not always lived up to the best of their own tradition in this regard. Many people still remember the moralistic transmission of dogma they received at school and rightly resist the coercive methods used in times past. Today, Catholic religious education invites children to investigate, interpret and analyse religious concepts and to apply them to their own lives in such a way that they don't just learn 'about' religion but they learn 'from' religion for their lives in the world. To enable children to become literate in their own religion, in this manner, helps them avoid the dangers of fundamentalism, sectarianism and ritualism on the one hand, and the dangers of relativism, apathy and a vague religiosity on the other.

... If you want your child to be autonomous in his/ her moral life

There is a developing consensus today on the importance of a strong initial formation as an essential component in a balanced education. This is the idea that it is good for children to be initiated into a particular set of beliefs, practices and values before they can begin to expand their horizons beyond the present and the particular. Children's emotional, cognitive and spiritual development depends upon their relationships in early childhood and there needs to be a sense of order in their world that they can trust. They benefit

---

14 Dermot A. Lane, 'Catholic Education and the Primary School in the Twenty-First Century', *Catholic Primary Education: Facing New Challenges* Eugene Duffy, ed. (Dublin: Columba Press, 2012). See *Decree on Religious Freedom* (1965), articles 2 and 9 respectively.

from having a stable and coherent ethical upbringing and that their prospects for developing moral autonomy are enhanced by enabling them to develop a strong ethical framework.

Ian MacMullen is one strong proponent of the argument that the development of autonomy in morality depends on the child being empowered to develop a coherent ethical framework as a child. He argues that in primary school, moral education is involved in getting children to hold particular beliefs and to behave in particular ways. It will be later that different points of view and the controversies that surround them should be introduced.[15] As MacMullen explains:

> before children have the cognitive capacity to engage in authentically autonomous ethical reflection, their long-run interest in developing autonomy is best served by consolidating their sense of identity within a coherent primary culture and beginning to teach the practice of ethical reasoning within the framework provided by that secure cultural identity.[16]

According to MacMullen, children's chances of developing moral autonomy are not served by exposing children to multiple ethical perspectives at a young age, but by encouraging critical engagement with the particular ethical perspective around which the school is constructed. So, for example, when teaching young children about the actions of Jesus, they will be asked to judge if he was right in what he did, whether it was good that he did it, and why. This kind of moral education introduces children to the kind of critical judgement required for autonomous moral living. At a later stage children will then be able to compare their own ethical framework with the other ethical frameworks available in their society.

---

15 Ian MacMullen, 'Education for Autonomy: the Role of Religious Elementary Schools', *Journal of Philosophy of Education* 38.4 (2004), p. 607.
16 Ibid., p. 610.

The Catholic school honours children's right to develop a coherent moral framework which takes their religious identity seriously.[17] This involves inviting children to grow in awareness of their identity as persons created in the image and likeness of God and called to live in loving, respectful relationship with God, other human persons and the whole of creation. They are introduced to Jesus as a model for living an ethical life and to the moral teachings of the Church that teach them how to live as his disciples. They learn the importance of prayer, asceticism and the sacraments in nurturing their moral lives. They learn to cultivate an upright and informed conscience and develop their ability for moral reasoning as they confront moral dilemmas. Some notable virtues, values and attitudes of the Christian tradition which are taught in the Catholic school include: the theological virtues (faith, hope, love); the cardinal virtues (prudence, justice, fortitude and temperance); gratitude, joy and forgiveness; respect for truth, compassion, justice, interdependence; respect for God, self and others; fair-mindedness, integrity, appreciation and wonder; enquiry and critical thought; social awareness and moral responsibility; confidence in one's own religious identity while valuing difference and diversity; acceptance of one's own fallibility, and appreciation of the sacred dimension of everyday life.

... If you want your child to belong to a Christian community

Catholics believe that human beings are not isolated individuals but persons who are essentially relational: I become a person only in and through my relationship to another. Every human being is called to communion because they have been created in the image

---

17 On children's right to religion as a challenge to educational 'neutrality', see Friedrich Schweitzer, 'Children's Right to Religion and Spirituality', *British Journal of Religious Education* 27.2 (2005), pp. 103–13.

and likeness of that communion of love that is the very life of God (Trinity). In the Catholic school children are invited to see themselves as part of a peoplehood and community that reaches backward in time and outwards towards all of humanity, and to see themselves as being connected with all people of faith redeemed by Christ down through the ages. As Eoin Cassidy explains,

> to be a Catholic is to accept that one is first and foremost a member of a community, and that one's life is defined in terms of one's membership of that community; one only becomes a spiritual person, someone who is in touch with oneself, to the extent that one is in touch with another … it is only in listening to another that one finds the key that will unlock the door to either one's own heart or to the presence of God in one's life, someone who, as Augustine never tired of preaching, is closer to me than I am to myself.[18]

There is an important difference here between philosophies of education that presume that human beings are first and foremost individuals and the Catholic claim that human nature is essentially interpersonal. One implication of this understanding is that education is seen not primarily as a means of material prosperity and success, but as that which will enable the person to serve and be responsible for others.[19] In the Catholic view, we journey to God together, by caring for ourselves and the people we live with and, in particular, by being ethically concerned for the poor.

---

18 Eoin G. Cassidy, 'Journeying Towards the "Other": A Challenge for Religious, Spiritual and Moral Education', *International Handbook*, M. de Souza et al, eds., pp. 871, 883.

19 Congregation for Catholic Education, *The Catholic School* (1977), n. 57.

... If you want your child to be able to engage positively with people of other religions and stances for living

The way in which Christians experience God involves an encounter with the self and with others, including people who are different from ourselves. To be Catholic means to be open to the saving action of God wherever it may be found. Catholics affirm the inclusivity and diversity of God's family by remaining open to the diversity and richness of both Christian and non-Christian traditions. Thomas H. Groome summarises this understanding of catholicity as inclusivity in the following manner:

> Becoming a Catholic Christian means growing to love and care for all humankind – cherishing their diversity, relishing life and maturing into its fullness – for oneself and others, embracing the world as gift and responsibility – convinced that you can make a difference for life for all ... It requires letting go of parochialism to embrace everyone as brother and sister, replacing narrow-mindedness with openness to learn from those who are very different ... A true Catholic is convinced that God loves every person equally and God's family embraces all humankind.[20]

Today, children are taught that being Catholic entails having a profound respect for and a willingness to dialogue with people of other religions and worldviews. Children are invited to learn about and from the religions of people in their communities, developing the attitudes and capacities that will enable them both to co-operate with their neighbours and respond to the ethical challenges of living with difference. A deep appreciation of Christianity provides the foundation for understanding of other religions and worldviews.

---

20 Thomas H. Groome, *Educating for Life* (Allen, Texas: Thomas More, 1998), p. 394.

Finally, children are taught that the Church reproves discrimination against people on the basis of race, colour or religion, and that Catholics are called to extend 'respect and love' to those who think or act differently than they do in religious matters.[21]

... If you want your child to have a strong sense of social justice and to contribute to the common good

The Catholic school is committed to preparing children to take an active role in social life as good citizens who promote the good of all people in society. They are formed in such a way as to respect the identity, culture, history, religion, human rights and especially the suffering and needs of others, conscious that 'we are all really responsible for all'.[22] As the Congregation for Catholic Education observes:

> Basically, the school is called to be a living witness of the love of God among us. It can, moreover, become a means through which it is possible to discern, in the light of the gospel, what is positive in the world, what needs to be transformed and what injustices must be overcome.[23]

At an early age, children are taught that the Church has a special mission to the poor, the sick and the marginalised. They are helped to develop an ethic that respects, defends and promotes the rights and wellbeing of every person regardless of gender, race, social status, personal achievement or social contribution. They are invited to consider their lives as a vocation and that they have a unique role to play in bringing about a more just and equitable world. This concern

---

21 Pope Paul VI, *Nostra Aetate* (1965), n. 5; *Gaudium et Spes* (1965), n. 28.

22 Congregation for Catholic Education, *Education Together in Catholic Schools* (2007), n. 44.

23 Ibid., n. 46.

for a more just world extends to all of creation as children are taught to contemplate and respect the earth in all its complexity and beauty. They are encouraged to develop reverence for all creation as a manifestation of the divine. Finally, they are enabled to develop an ecological conscience which calls for prophetic challenges to forces destroying the earth.

Conclusion

Offer your child the gift of Catholic religious education if you ...

» believe that God is God of *all* life both here and hereafter;
» want your child to learn how to follow Jesus in living his life;
» want your child to have a sense of him or herself as something more than the sum of his or her achievements, looks, possessions and gifts;
» believe that the greatest gift you could give your child is the discovery of his or her spiritual depths and divine identity;
» want to gift your child with the art of using Christian religious language to give a deeper meaning to his or her life in the world;
» believe that with a strong ethical framework, a sense of social justice and a genuine openness towards all those he or she encounters in life, your child might thereby continue the good in your life.

Contributors

Michael Drumm is chairperson of the Catholic Schools' Partnership, an association established by the Irish Bishops' Conference and the Conference of Religious of Ireland. Its aims are to foster coherence in Catholic education at a national level, provide a unified voice for Catholic education in the public forum and with educational bodies and the government, support Catholic educators in the core activities of learning and teaching in order to foster high-quality, life-long learning and faith development for all learners, and support the roles of governance, trusteeship and management. A priest of the diocese of Elphin and former director of Mater Dei Institute of Education, Dublin, he is the author of several books and articles on sacramental theology.

Anne Hession is a lecturer in Religious Studies and Religious Education at St Patrick's College, a college of Dublin City University. She is an experienced teacher at both primary and tertiary levels. A graduate of Boston College, she is the co-author with Patricia Kieran of *Children, Catholicism and Religious Education* (2005); and co-editor with Patricia Kieran of *Exploring Theology* (2007) and *Exploring Religious Education* (2008). Since 2010, she has been working on the Catholic Preschool and Primary School Curriculum (forthcoming).

Amalee Meehan, PhD Boston College, taught with Coláiste Iognáid, Galway, before joining Catholic Education, an Irish Schools Trust (CEIST), where she works in faith leadership and governance. She teaches on the MA Christian Leadership in Education with Mary Immaculate College, University of Limerick, and is the co-author of two religious education textbooks for US Catholic High Schools as part of the *Credo* series (Veritas, ongoing).

Bishop Donal McKeown was ordained as a priest for the diocese of Down and Connor in 1977 and taught for twenty-three years, including six years as school principal. In 2001 he was ordained Titular Bishop of Killossy and Auxiliary to the Bishop of Down and Connor. He is a member of the Episcopal Council for Worship, Pastoral Renewal and Faith Development, member of the Council for Clergy, Chairman of the Council for Vocations, member of the Council for Pastoral Renewal and Adult Faith Development, Chair of Committee for Youth and Young Adult Ministry, and a member of the Council for Education of the Irish Catholic Bishops' Conference.

Baroness Nuala O'Loan DBE, MRIA is a member of the UK House of Lords. She is chair of the governing authority of NUI Maynooth. She was Ireland's Roving Ambassador for Conflict Resolution and Special Envoy to Timor Leste. She works with the International Contact Group Basque Country in Spain. She was the Police Ombudsman for Northern Ireland, responsible for criminal and other investigation of the police. She has chaired and served on public bodies in areas as diverse as the European Union, health, transport, policing, human rights and energy. She writes on justice, policing, and faith, speaks regularly across the world, and has acted in an advisory capacity to government agencies responsible for policing and police accountability, in Africa, Asia, India, Europe and North and South America. She is married to Declan O'Loan MLA and they have five sons.

John-Paul Sheridan is a priest of the diocese of Ferns, a curate at the parish of St Brigid, Blackwater, Co. Wexford, and a Diocesan Advisor for Primary School Catechetics. He frequently speaks to parents and parishes, lectures intermittently on religious education and catechesis and is the author of *Promises to Keep: Parents and Confirmation* (2004). He is a PhD graduate of Trinity College, Dublin, where his research was concerned with the religious identity of primary school student teachers.

Orla Walsh is a Faith Development Officer for the Spiritan Education Trust (DEA). She is the author of *Angels for Little People* (2006), *Searching* (2006), *Know The Way* (2007) and *FaithConnect* (2009). Orla is a graduate of Mater Dei Institute of Education and is currently working on a professional doctorate there in conjunction with the School of Education Studies, Dublin City University. Her interests include adolescent spirituality in a contemporary context and the creative imagination as a motivation in faith. Orla lives in Trim, Co. Meath, with her husband, Barry, two sons, Oisín and Cian, and her daughter, Aoise.